Modern Critical Interpretations

William Shakespeare's Antony and Cleopatra

Modern Critical Interpretations

These and other titles in preparation

Modern Critical Interpretations

William Shakespeare's
Antony and Cleopatra

Edited and with an introduction by
Harold Bloom
Sterling Professor of the Humanities
Yale University

Chelsea House Publishers ◇ *1988*
NEW YORK ◇ NEW HAVEN ◇ PHILADELPHIA

© 1988 by Chelsea House Publishers, a division
of Chelsea House Educational Communications, Inc.,
  95 Madison Avenue, New York, NY 10016
  345 Whitney Avenue, New Haven, CT 06511
  5068B West Chester Pike, Edgemont, PA 19028

Introduction © 1988 by Harold Bloom

Printed and bound in the United States of America

10 9 8 7 6 5 4 3 2 1

∞ The paper used in this publication meets the minimum
requirements of the American National Standard for Permanence
of Paper for Printed Library Materials, Z39.48–1984.

Library of Congress Cataloging-in-Publication Data
William Shakespeare's Antony and Cleopatra.
  (Modern critical interpretations)
  Bibliography: p. 173
  Includes index.
  1. Shakespeare, William, 1564–1616. Antony and
Cleopatra. I. Bloom, Harold. II. Title: Antony and
Cleopatra. III. Series.
PR2802.W55 1988   822.3'3   87-18229
ISBN 0-87754-921-4

Contents

Editor's Note

This book brings together a representative selection of the best modern critical interpretations of William Shakespeare's *The Tragedy of Antony and Cleopatra*. The critical essays are reprinted here in the chronological order of their original publication.

My introduction centers upon the deaths of Antony and of Cleopatra, with particular emphasis upon her astonishing transmutation as the representation of a consciousness. Janet Adelman begins the chronological sequence with her brilliant analysis of the dialectic of character and knowledge in the play.

In Anne Barton's reading, we are shown how the play always directs us back to Cleopatra's complex perspectives. Rosalie L. Colie's essay turns on Shakespeare's alternation of plain and hyperbolic styles, so as to suggest "the strength, the vividness, the vigor of excess which this play presents."

Shakespearean representation, with its unique power of accomplishing an effect always beyond modernity, is the subject of Howard Felperin's study of *Antony and Cleopatra*. John Bayley gives us an exegesis of the fine balance between romance and realism that is maintained throughout the drama.

Our contemporary critical awareness of the problematics of gender enters with Linda Bamber's feminist argument that the fame Antony and Cleopatra earn from their connection with each other "depends on the space between them." Another current mode, "cultural materialism," is represented here by Jonathan Dollimore's description of how *Antony and Cleopatra* "celebrates . . . not the love which transcends power but the sexual infatuation which foregrounds it."

This book concludes with Laura Quinney's superb essay on the antithetical languages of intimacy and isolation in the play. Published here for the first time, Quinney's essay seems to me a model instance of precisely how the most advanced contemporary criticism can retain an archaic sense that there is an element in the strongest poetry that cannot be reduced to our ongoing critical polemics, our resentments and irritations as to the supposed divisions of gender, class, history, rank, and power.

Introduction

Freud taught us that the therapy-of-therapies is not to invest too much libido in any single object whosoever. Antony at last refuses this wisdom and in consequence suffers what must be called an erotic tragedy, but then Cleopatra, who has spent her life exemplifying the same wisdom, suffers an erotic tragedy also, on Antony's account, one act of the drama more belatedly than he does. *The Tragedy of Antony and Cleopatra* is unique among Shakespeare's plays in that the tragedy's doubleness, equal in both man and woman as it was with Romeo and Juliet, takes place between equally titanic personages. Each truly is all but everything in himself and herself, and *knows* it, and neither fears that he or she is really nothing in himself or herself, or nothing without the other. Both consciously play many parts, and yet also *are* those other parts. Both are adept at playing themselves, yet also at being themselves. Like Falstaff and Hamlet, they are supreme personalities, major wits, grand counter-Machiavels (though overmatched by Octavian, greatest of Machiavels), and supreme consciousnesses. They fall in love with one another, resist and betray the love repeatedly, but finally yield to it and are destroyed by it, in order fully to fulfill their allied natures. More even than the death of Hamlet, we react to their suicides as a human triumph and as a release for ourselves. But why? And how?

The crucial originality here is to have represented two great personalities, the Herculean hero proper and a woman of infinite guile and resource, in their overwhelming decline and mingled ruin. A destruction through authentic and mutual love becomes an aesthetic redemption precisely because love's shadow is ruin. We have no representations of this kind before Shakespeare, since a Euripidean vision of erotic ruin, as in the *Medea*, permits no aesthetic redemption, while Virgil's Dido, like Medea, is a solitary sufferer. Antony and Cleopatra repeatedly betray one another, and betray themselves, yet these betrayals are forgiven by them and by us, since they become phases of apotheosis that release the sparks of grandeur even as the lamps are shattered.

From act 4, scene 14, through to the end of the play, we hear something wonderfully original even for Shakespeare, a great dying fall, the release of a new music. It begins with the dialogue between Antony and his marvelously named, devoted follower, Eros:

ANTONY. Eros, thou yet behold'st me?
EROS.   Ay, noble lord.
ANTONY. Sometime we see a cloud that's dragonish,
    A vapor sometime like a bear or lion,
    A [tower'd] citadel, a pendant rock,
    A forked mountain, or blue promontory
    With trees upon't that nod unto the world,
    And mock our eyes with air. Thou hast seen these signs,
    They are black vesper's pageants.
EROS.   Ay, my lord.
ANTONY. That which is now a horse, even with a thought
    The rack dislimns, and makes it indistinct
    As water is in water.
EROS.   It does, my lord.
ANTONY. My good knave Eros, now thy captain is
    Even such a body. Here I am Antony,
    Yet cannot hold this visible shape, my knave.
    I made these wars for Egypt, and the Queen,
    Whose heart I thought I had, for she had mine—
    Which whilst it was mine had annex'd unto't
    A million moe (now lost)—she, Eros, has
    Pack'd cards with Caesar's, and false-play'd my glory
    Unto an enemy's triumph.
    Nay, weep not, gentle Eros, there is left us
    Ourselves to end ourselves.

There is a deliberate touch of the cloud-watching Hamlet in Antony here, but with Hamlet's parodistic savagery modulated into a gentleness that befits the transmutation of the charismatic hero into a self-transcendent consciousness, almost beyond the consolations of farewell. The grandeur of this transformation is enhanced when Antony receives the false tidings Cleopatra sends of her supposed death, with his name her last utterance:

> Unarm, Eros, the long day's task is done,
> And we must sleep.

The answering chorus to that splendor is Cleopatra's, when he dies in her arms:

> The crown o'th'earth doth melt. My lord!
> O, wither'd is the garland of the war,
> The soldier's pole is fall'n! Young boys and girls
> Are level now with men; the odds is gone,
> And there is nothing left remarkable
> Beneath the visiting moon.

Antony touches the Sublime as he prepares to die, but Cleopatra's lament for a lost Sublime is the prelude to a greater sublimity, which is to be wholly her own. She is herself a great actress, so that the difficulty in playing her, for any actress, is quite extraordinary. And though she certainly loved Antony, it is inevitable that, like any great actress, she must love herself all but apocalyptically. Antony has a largeness about him surpassing any other Shakespearean hero except for Hamlet; he is an ultimate version of the charismatic leader, loved and followed because his palpable glory can be shared, in some degree, since he is also magnificently generous. But Shakespeare shrewdly ends him with one whole act of the play to go, and retrospectively we see that the drama is as much Cleopatra's as the two parts of *Henry IV* are Falstaff's.

Remarkable as Antony is in himself, he interests us primarily because he has the splendor that makes him as much a catastrophe for Cleopatra as she is for him. Cleopatra is in love with his exuberance, with the preternatural vitality that impresses even Octavian. But she knows, as we do, that Antony lacks her infinite variety. Their love, in Freudian terms, is not narcissistic but anaclitic; they are propped upon one another, cosmological beings who are likely to be bored by any-one else, by any personality neither their own nor one another's. Antony is Cleopatra's only true match and yet he is not her equal, which may be the most crucial or deepest meaning of the play. An imaginative being in that he moves the imagination of others, he is simply not an imaginer of her stature. He need not play himself; he is Herculean. Cleopatra ceases to play herself only when she is trans-muted by his death and its aftermath, and we cannot be sure, even then, that she is not both performing and simultaneously becoming that more transcendent self. Strangely like the dying Hamlet in this single respect, she suggests, at the end, that she stands upon a new threshold of being:

> I am fire and air; my other elements
> I give to baser life.

Is she no longer the earth of Egypt, or the water of the Nile? We have not exactly thought of her as a devoted mother, despite her children by Julius Caesar and by Antony, but in her dying dialogue with Charmian she transmutes the asps, first into her baby, and then apparently into an Antony she might have brought to birth, as in some sense indeed she did:

> CHARMIAN. O eastern star!
> CLEOPATRA.   Peace, peace!
>   Dost thou not see my baby at my breast,
>   That sucks the nurse asleep?
> CHARMIAN.   O, break! O, break!
> CLEOPATRA. As sweet as balm, as soft as air, as gentle—O
>   Antony!—Nay, I will take thee too:
>   [Applying another asp to her arm.]
>   What should I stay—   Dies.

As Lear dies, Kent cries out "Break, heart, I prithee break!" even as Charmian does here, not wishing upon the rack of this tough world to stretch Cleopatra out longer. When Antony's men find him wounded to death, they lament that "the star is fall'n," and that "time is at his period." Charmian's "O eastern star!" associates one dying lover with the other, even as her echo of Kent suggests that the dying Empress of the East is in something like the innocence of Lear's madness. Cleopatra is sucked to sleep as a mother is by a child, or a woman by a lover, and dies in such peace that Octavian, of all men, is moved to the ultimate tribute:

> she looks like sleep,
> As she would catch another Antony
> In her strong toil of grace.

Bewildering us by her final manifestation of her infinite variety, Cleopatra dies into a beyond, a Sublime where actress never trod.

Infinite Variety: Uncertainty and Judgment in *Antony and Cleopatra*

Janet Adelman

The critical history of *Antony and Cleopatra* can be seen largely as a series of attempts to assess the motives of the protagonists and to arbitrate between the claims of Egypt and Rome. But this search for certainty often encounters the stumbling block of the play itself: at almost every turn, there are significant lapses in our knowledge of the inner state of the principal characters; and we cannot judge what we do not know. The characters themselves continually tell us that they do not know one another, that their judgments are fallible. Nor can we attribute the critics' persistent search for answers merely to their stubbornness: for the play demands that we make judgments even as it frustrates our ability to judge rationally. This frustration is not an end in itself: it forces us to participate in the experience of the play and ultimately to make the same leap of faith that the lovers make. In this sense, our uncertainty is an essential feature of the play.

The moral of recent Shakespeare criticism may be that any tragedy studied long enough reveals that it deliberately provokes uncertainty; and in fact, there are some mysteries of plot, motivation, value, and judgment in all of them. But in other plays, we are usually certain of a few central facts; and we usually have our moral bearings. Despite our doubts about the ghost, we know that Claudius killed old Hamlet. We may question the value of vengeance or of any action in a corrupt state, but our questioning does not usually shake our conviction that

From *The Common Liar: An Essay on* Antony and Cleopatra. © 1973 by Yale University. Yale University Press, 1973.

the state must be set right. Despite the foolish irascibility of the old king or the foolish credulity of the Moor, we know who is right in *King Lear* or *Othello*; despite Macbeth's eloquent grandeur, we are morally satisfied when he is killed by Macduff. But no such satisfaction awaits us in *Antony and Cleopatra*, where both the presentation of character and the dramatic structure work to frustrate our reasonable desire for certainty. Certainty, even of a limited kind, seems essential to the tragic experience. But *Antony and Cleopatra* is only partly tragic; or at least the tragic vision is subject to the same questioning as everything else in the play.

CHARACTER AND KNOWLEDGE

Not know me yet?
(3.13.157)

Although the play continually raises questions about motives, it simply does not give any clear answers to them. Almost every major action in the play is in some degree inexplicable. Why did Antony marry Octavia if he planned to return to Cleopatra? Was Octavius ruthless or merely blind in his plan to marry his sister to Antony? Does Antony return to the East for love of Cleopatra or because his spirit is overpowered when he is near Octavius? As the play progresses, the questions accumulate around Cleopatra; and they become more urgent. Is Cleopatra merely exercising her powers over Thidias for the sake of the game, or does she really hope to woo Octavius through him? Is her scene with Seleucus a cunningly staged device to convince Octavius that she has no desire to die, or does she in fact have hopes of a future life without Antony in which some lady trifles will be useful? Even the most critical action in the plot goes unexplained: Antony has won a victory against Octavius and regained the loyalty of his own men (a victory greatly magnified in importance from the account in Plutarch); but in the next encounter, his fleet yields to Octavius and his defeat is certain. Did the ships join with Octavius under Cleopatra's orders, as Antony assumes? If not, then who is responsible for this final betrayal of Antony? These questions are not all equally unanswerable; and our preferences and critical ingenuity will usually combine with the text of the play to produce satisfactory answers to most of them. But most of the time the answers will satisfy only ourselves. I for one am as unwilling to imagine a fundamentally disloyal Cleopatra as the most romantic critic and will argue for the best possible interpretation of her actions; but the fact is that the play will support the arguments of my opponents almost as readily as mine. We simply are not told the motives of the protagonists at the most critical points in the action.

Shakespeare was not accustomed to leaving his audience entirely in the dark on central issues in his tragedies. We may not know why Lear chooses to divide his kingdom so arbitrarily; but once we have accepted the initial situation, we are given frequent insights into his mind through his own soliloquies and asides and through a technique of projection called "umbrella speeches" by Maynard Mack, in which the fool, for instance, serves "as a screen on which Shakespeare flashes, as it were, readings from the psychic life of the protagonists." But in *Antony and Cleopatra,* the only major soliloquy is Enobarbus's; and the asides are almost exclusively the property of the minor characters. Antony does tell us in soliloquy of his determination to return to the East (2.3) and of his rage and love for Cleopatra (4.12; 4.14); but these speeches are by no means the meditations on his own inner state which we associate with soliloquy in the major tragedies. Moreover, the "umbrella speeches" and speeches by other characters which seem to reflect the state of the protagonists accurately often turn out upon examination to be wrong. No play in which the characters remain so essentially opaque to each other and to the audience can satisfy us in the way of *Macbeth*—in the way, that is, of character revelation and moral certainty.

There are, of course, moments at which the characters are opaque in the other tragedies, but these mysteries are, I think, of a slightly different order. Generations of critics have argued, for instance, about why Hamlet does not kill the king while he is praying. Is it really because he does not want to send Claudius's soul to heaven, or must we look deeper into Hamlet's character toward those philosophic or psychoanalytic scruples which keep him from action altogether? We must note that Hamlet himself gives us a perfectly good reason for not killing Claudius praying: that heaven is no recompense for hell. Although we may choose (at our peril) to disbelieve his reason, it is at any rate evident that Hamlet believes it. Moreover, we are informed at this critical moment of the process of Hamlet's mind: although we may feel that we have not been told the whole truth, at least the illusion of insight into Hamlet's motivation has been given by the soliloquy. If an aura of mystery persists nonetheless, it is perhaps because the literary figure in this instance creates so absolute an illusion of reality that he breeds all the mysteries of character which we find in real life. The sense of opaqueness comes more from the success of the illusion than from any failure to explicate character: Shakespeare gives us insight into Hamlet's inner state at virtually every turn in the play.

A fully realized character like Hamlet will necessarily appear mysterious at some moments precisely insofar as he is fully realized; a relatively unrealized character like Iago will engender mysteries of another sort. Iago's frequent soliloquies reveal his motives and his machinations: Cassio has got the job he wanted; he suspects both Cassio and Othello of cuckolding him; and the daily beauty of Cassio's life makes his own ugly. But the more motives Iago gives us, the less likely they seem as explanations of his actions. His motives do not seem equal to the deed, nor can they account for that fundamental hatred of life and love of contrivance which rule him. "I hate the Moor," he says, and then explicitly denies that he hates him for any particular reason:

> And it is thought abroad, that 'twixt my sheets
> He's done my office; I know not if't be true . . .
> Yet I, for mere suspicion in that kind,
> Will do, as if for surety.
>
> (1.3.385–88)

We are not here fundamentally concerned with Iago's character; mere ordinary human motivation is serving as the excuse for some more essential hatred which it surely could not have caused. Our impression, despite the soliloquies and their revelation of motivation, is not that the byways of Iago's character have been revealed to us but rather that essential evil of Iago's sort is a self-perpetuating, self-aggrandizing, and finally self-annihilating machine to which motivation is almost wholly irrelevant after the initial move is made. We become more interested in watching the diabolical principle at work in a human being than in the character of Iago per se and his inconsistent motivation. It is with a similar disinterest in the intricacies of character that we watch the redemptive principle working through Cordelia. Figures like Iago or Cordelia tend to function less as fully realized characters than as embodiments of moral principles. And in proportion as they are less fully human than Hamlet, as they are more purely symbolic, we are less interested in their inner states. They can afford to be opaque because we are not fundamentally interested in them as characters: mysteries of motivation simply evaporate insofar as they take their places as parts of a symbolic action.

But in *Antony and Cleopatra,* the protagonists neither reveal their motives to us nor are they content merely to take their places in a symbolic action. They create the same sort of illusion of reality that Hamlet creates but do not give us even the partial insights into their souls that Hamlet gives. We are forced to concern ourselves with their characters as we are not with Iago's or Cordelia's; and yet their characters remain opaque. True, a desire to understand character in the play may be dismissed by some modern critics as naive; and there is little question that *Antony and Cleopatra* becomes a more unified and explicable whole if it is read as a lyric poem or an allegory to which questions of character are largely irrelevant. But we may not be able to believe entirely in the play-as-lyric-poem of Knight and Knights or in the character-as-a-bundle-of-stage-conventions of Schücking and Stoll or in the character-as-symbol of Bethell; or at least these theories may not be able to explain away character altogether. However convincing they are in part, they do not quite allay the nagging suspicion that the illusion of character is in some measure relevant to drama, and particularly to this one. Critics have persisted in trying to find answers to the questions of motivation and emotion in *Antony and Cleopatra;* and though questions of character may occasionally be irrelevant, this critical persistence suggests that they are not irrelevant here. If the same questions are continually asked, then I think we must conclude that the questions have been elicited by the play; the search is interminable not because the questions are wrong but because the answers are not given.

To explain character away, and with it the unanswerable questions, is in this instance to explain the play away: for the whole play can be seen as a series of attempts on the parts of the characters to understand and judge each other and themselves. We see Cleopatra dallying with Thidias in act 3, scene 13: Enobarbus thinks he sees Cleopatra betraying Antony and transferring her allegiance to Caesar; Antony thinks he sees the operations of lascivious habit. What have they seen? Do we watch a cunning queen outfox a wily politician in the scene with Seleucus, or a servant betray his mistress? This uncertainty is apparent not only in the critical moments of the play (did Cleopatra's ships join Caesar's on her orders?) but during numerous small scenes. And we are as baffled as the characters; like them, we see only the bare event and are left to speculate upon its meaning.

Throughout the play, the characters themselves question its meaning for us; the questioning is so habitual that it occurs explicitly even in those relatively minor scenes where the meaning does not seem to be at issue. When the soothsayer tells Charmian that she shall be far fairer than she is, the two women debate his meaning:

> CHARMIAN. He means in flesh.
> IRAS. No, you shall paint when you are old.
>
> (1.2.17–18)

Their debate is poignant because neither can guess the true meaning of his prophecies. The question of meaning is most explicitly raised in the small scene in which Antony bids his servants farewell; there it is raised four times in thirty-five lines. We would expect Cleopatra to know Antony as well as anyone; yet she asks Enobarbus, "What means this?" (4.2.13) and, ten lines later, "What does he mean?" Enobarbus then asks Antony directly: "What mean you, sir, / To give them this discomfort?" (ll. 33–34). Antony immediately denies that he meant his words as Enobarbus and the servants have taken them:

> Ho, ho, ho!
> Now the witch take me, if I meant it thus!
> Grace grow where those drops fall, my hearty friends;
> You take me in too dolorous a sense,
> For I spake to you for your comfort.
>
> (4.2.36–40)

Antony's attempt to console his followers by rearranging his meaning explicitly raises the issue of interpretation; even here, we are faced with one of the central dilemmas of the play. Virtually the only way out of this dilemma is the way that Antony takes at the end of the scene, when he in effect plays Horatio to his own Hamlet: "Let's to supper, come, / And drown consideration" (ll. 44–45). In the scene which follows immediately, we are shown another farewell embedded in controversy:

> SECOND SOLDIER. Heard you of nothing strange about the streets?
> FIRST SOLDIER. Nothing: what news?
> SECOND SOLDIER. Belike 'tis but a rumour.
>
> (4.3.3–5)

The rumor is of course instantly verified: the music of Hercules departing is heard and debated.

FOURTH SOLDIER. It signs well, does it not?

THIRD SOLDIER.   No.

FIRST SOLDIER.   Peace, I say:

    What should this mean?

SECOND SOLDIER. 'Tis the god Hercules, whom Antony lov'd,

    Now leaves him.

(4.3.13–16)

Nothing goes unquestioned in this play. In most literature there is a convention that character is knowable as it rarely is in life, that characters act in accordance with certain constant, recognizable, and explicable principles which we and they can know. This convention does not operate in *Antony and Cleopatra*. There the characters do not know each other, nor can we know them, any more clearly than we know ourselves. In the midst of Antony's rage against Cleopatra and Thidias, Cleopatra asks him, "Not know me yet?" (3.12.157). Antony can scarcely be blamed for not knowing Cleopatra; the question stands as central to the play. From Cleopatra's "If it be love indeed, tell me how much" (1.1.14) to the First Guardsman's "Is this well done?" (5.2.324), questions of motive, of value, and of the truth of the emotions are insistently raised. Emotions are unreliable and constantly changing; characters question their own emotions as well as those of others. From the beginning we see Cleopatra stage emotions for Antony's benefit ("If you find him sad, / Say I am dancing" [1.3.3–4]; "I am sick, and sullen" [1.3.13]). She accuses Antony of playacting his rage ("You can do better yet; but this is meetly" [1.3.81]). We know that Antony "married but his occasion" (2.6.128) in marrying Octavia, for he himself tells us, "I make this marriage for my peace" (2.3.38). But what of Fulvia? "Why did he marry Fulvia, and not love her?" (1.1.41). Even Antony muses on his inconstant emotions: "she's good, being gone, / The hand could pluck her back that shov'd her on" (1.2.123–24). Is Antony's emotion love indeed? Cleopatra asks, "Why should I think you can be mine and true . . . / Who have been false to Fulvia?" (1.3.27–29). Why indeed? Antony thinks Cleopatra's passions are feigned: "She is cunning past man's thought" (1.2.143). But Enobarbus answers that "her passions are made of nothing but the finest parts of pure love" (1.2.144–45); and whatever his tone of voice, his words at least contradict Antony's. Enobarbus and Agrippa mock Lepidus's protestations of love for both Antony and Caesar (3.2). Cleopatra idly asks, "Did I, Charmian, / Ever love Caesar so?" (1.5.66–67), and is most displeased with Charmian's teasing answer.

The tears wept by Antony's crocodile are characteristic of this persistent questioning of emotion. Cleopatra assumes that Antony will weep crocodile tears for her: "I prithee turn aside and weep for her, / Then bid adieu to me, and say the tears / Belong to Egypt" (1.3.76–78). "The tears live in an onion, that should water this sorrow" (1.2.167–68), Enobarbus says of Fulvia's death; yet even when Enobarbus is genuinely moved by Antony's farewell to his servants, he calls himself "onion-ey'd" (4.2.35). When Caesar weeps at parting from Octavia, Agrippa recalls Antony's tears:

> When Antony found Julius Caesar dead,
> He cried almost to roaring; and he wept
> When at Philippi he found Brutus slain.
> (3.2.54–56)

Characteristically, Enobarbus points the moral:

> That year, indeed, he was troubled with a rheum;
> What willingly he did confound, he wail'd,
> Believe't, till I wept too.
> (3.2.57–59)

Antony's weeping over Brutus recalls his sorrow over Fulvia; in both instances he grieves for what he himself has helped to destroy. The movement is characteristic of the play: we shall see Caesar too weep at what willingly he did confound when Decretas reports Antony's death ("The gods rebuke me, but it is a tidings / To wash the eyes of kings" 5.1.27–28); Agrippa comments upon the inconsistency of the emotion much as Enobarbus and Antony have already commented ("And strange it is, / That nature must compel us to lament / Our most persisted deeds" [5.1.28–30]). During Cleopatra's suicide, Charmian asks in effect for cosmic crocodile tears, for the show of cosmic grief: "Dissolve, thick cloud, and rain, that I may say, / The gods themselves do weep!" (5.2.298–99).

The full acknowledgement of all this uncertainty is in Antony's quiet lines, "I made these wars for Egypt, and the queen, / Whose heart I thought I had, for she had mine" (4.14.15–16). Does Antony have her heart? Or does she too discover that Antony is good only when he is gone? In the end, the uncertainty implicates us as well as the characters: we must question Cleopatra's love for Antony as she plans her suicide;

Shakespeare's insistence upon her dread of a Roman triumph forces us to question it. But in this play, not even skepticism is a secure position: Enobarbus shows us that. He persistently questions the sincerity of the passions, but when he follows his reason, he dies of a broken heart. At his death, we who have agreed with his rational skepticism are at a loss: skepticism itself is no more reliable than passion. If we are finally convinced of Cleopatra's love—and I think we are—we have had to develop a faith nearly as difficult as Antony's, a faith in what we cannot know.

THE DILEMMA OF JUDGMENT

> *Though he be painted one way like a Gorgon,*
> *The other way's a Mars.*
>
> (2.5.116–17)

If we are forced to participate in this questioning of emotion, with all its consequences, we are also forced to participate in the act of judgment. The desire to judge and be judged correctly is one of the dominant passions of the play; it is no wonder that the critics have spent so long trying to judge between Rome and Egypt when the characters themselves are so concerned with right judgment. "Is Antony, or we, in fault for this?" (3.13.2), Cleopatra asks after Actium: it is another of those questions which seem central to our experience of the play. Enobarbus answers "Antony only" without hesitation; but he can afford to give this partial judgment because he had already condemned Cleopatra before the fact ("Your presence needs must puzzle Antony" [3.7.10]). Antony's desire to die nobly, Cleopatra's dread of a Roman triumph: both are part of this overriding concern with judgment. Throughout the play, we see people making images of themselves, rearranging their own story. Cleopatra virtually stage-manages her death; and Caesar tries to arrange for correct judgment of himself with nearly every word he speaks. When first we see him, he is busily justifying himself to Lepidus ("You may see, Lepidus, and henceforth know, / It is not Caesar's natural vice to hate / Our great competitor" [1.4.1–3]). His last words in the play are a judgment on the pity of the lovers' story and inevitably on his own glory ("their story is / No less in pity than his glory which / Brought them to be lamented" [5.2.359–61]). Enobarbus, that inveterate judge of others, dies judging himself as well as Antony:

>   O Antony,
> Nobler than my revolt is infamous,
> Forgive me in thine own particular,
> But let the world rank me in register
> A master-leaver, and a fugitive.
>
>   (4.9.18–22)

In a sense, the play is a series of conflicting judgments passed on the protagonists, even by the protagonists themselves. In the first scene Antony attempts to "bind, / On pain of punishment, the world to weet / We stand up peerless" (1.1.38–40); but the world is watching, in the form of Demetrius and Philo, and its judgment is quite otherwise. For in this play, no judgment is absolute. If we see Caesar's "old ruffian" (4.1.4), we also see Cleopatra's "man of men" (1.5.72); if we see "salt Cleopatra" (2.1.21), we also see "a lass unparallel'd" (5.2.315). Cleopatra herself calls attention to this conflict in judgments: "Though he be painted one way like a Gorgon, / The other way's a Mars" (2.5.116–17).

Argumentation is the central mode of the play; not even the Romans can agree with one another. The first words of the play are "Nay, but": enter Philo and Demetrius, arguing. We later see Enobarbus and Antony arguing about Cleopatra (1.2) and Caesar and Lepidus arguing about Antony (1.4). The habit of contrariness infects even the watchmen who oversee Enobarbus's death and quibble about whether he is asleep or has swooned. Throughout, one man's meat is another man's poison. There is no room here for a moral scheme which tidily apportions the world according to vices and virtues. In that sense, the basis for judgment is itself continually challenged. Enobarbus says that Cleopatra "did make defect perfection" (2.2.231): "vilest things / Become themselves in her" (2.2.238–39). Even the Romans describe the lovers as creatures beyond the reach of ordinary judgment. Lepidus defends Antony precisely by pointing out his faults:

>   I must not think there are
> Evils enow to darken all his goodness:
> His faults, in him, seem as the spots of heaven,
> More fiery by night's blackness.
>
>   (1.4.10–13)

A metaphor in which goodness is blackness and faults stars mitigates against the possibility of any simple moral judgment. Caesar himself is willing to grant for the sake of argument the vilest things may become Antony; he answers Lepidus,

> say this becomes him,—
> As his composure must be rare indeed
> Whom these things cannot blemish,—yet must Antony
> No way excuse his foils, when we do bear
> So great weight in his lightness.
>
> (1.4.21–25)

And if the lovers' defects may be their perfections, Enobarbus knows that Octavia's perfections may be defects in Antony's judgment (2.6. 117–23).

The very process of judging is unreliable: as Cleopatra's image of the perspective painting (2.5.116–17) suggests, judgment depends on where one stands. Pompey is quite certain that he knows the lovers and can judge them; and his judgment seems intended to persuade us that he is right. His great condemnation of the lovers is frequently cited as though it were Shakespeare's own judgment and one which we ought to share.

> Mark Antony
> In Egypt sits at dinner, and will make
> No wars without doors. . . .
>
> . . . .
>
> . . . but all the charms of love,
> Salt Cleopatra, soften thy wan'd lip!
> Let witchcraft join with beauty, lust with both,
> Tie up the libertine in a field of feasts,
> Keep his brain fuming; Epicurean cooks
> Sharpen with cloyless sauce his appetite,
> That sleep and feeding may prorogue his honour,
> Even till a Lethe'd dulness—
>
> (2.1.11–13, 20–27)

If other characters in disparate situations make the same observations, then we feel that the judgment is corroborated and hence trustworthy. Several elements in Pompey's judgment are in fact verified by the play. Antony himself suggests that Cleopatra is a witch: he has already called her "this enchanting queen" (1.2.125) and will later call her "this false soul of Egypt! this grave charm" (4.12.25). The fair field of feasts which Pompey evokes is described in some detail by Enobarbus in the next scene (2.2.127ff.); also in the next scene Antony admits to Caesar that his brain has occasionally been kept fuming by feasts ("Three kings had I newly feasted, and did want / Of what I was i' the morning" [2.2.76–77]). Consequently we must trust Pompey's judgment. Or must we? Pompey might have continued his diatribe forever if he had not been interrupted by a messenger at the very height of it. Pompey's eloquence is so great that too few critics have noticed an important detail: the messenger contradicts absolutely the judgment which Pompey has just delivered.

> POMPEY. Even till a Lethe'd dulness—
>   *Enter Varrius*
>
>   How now, Varrius?
> VARRIUS. This is most certain, that I shall deliver:
>   Mark Antony is every hour in Rome
>   Expected.
>
>   (2.1.27–30)

This is most certain indeed. Pompey's reply is a little weak: "I did not think / This amorous surfeiter would have donn'd his helm" (ll. 32–33). But this new piece of information does not cause Pompey to change his fundamental judgment of Antony: he is still "this amorous surfeiter" and "the ne'er-lust-wearied Antony" (l. 38) even when the messenger has just belied this judgment. Pompey's judgment asks us simultaneously to believe and disbelieve it: for an audience accustomed to knowing where it stands, this uncertainty is intolerable. And Pompey's judgment is in this sense typical of all judgments in *Antony and Cleopatra*: each tells us as much about the judge and his perspective as it does about the accused.

The degree to which we can rely on a character's judgment is often at issue in Shakespeare. Edgar's assessment of events in *King Lear* is generally undercut by the events themselves, perhaps most vehemently when his blinded father is led in immediately after he has pronounced that "the worst returns to laughter" (4.1.6). At the end of many of the tragedies we are given judgments which are significantly challenged by the play as a whole: we do not, for example, accept Malcolm's "this dead butcher and his fiend-like queen" (*Macbeth* 5.9.35) as the whole truth about Macbeth and Lady Macbeth. But in the other tragedies, there are usually some reliable judgments interspersed among those which are clearly partial. When Regan tells us that Lear "hath ever but slenderly known himself" (1.1.292), we accept her judgment, in spite of our distrust of the judge. And despite the occasional inaccuracies of judgment, the analogy of the perspective painting is wholly inappropriate to *Hamlet, Othello, King Lear*, or *Macbeth*; its inappropriateness is the measure of the distance between these plays and *Antony and Cleopatra*. In fact, part of the effect of the tragedies depends precisely on our ability to make moral judgments: that something is rotten in the state of Denmark, that Desdemona is chaste and Iago evil, that Lear is more sinned against than sinning. But in *Antony and Cleopatra* we frequently find that we can make no judgment at all, or that our judgments are no more reliable than Pompey's.

Our involvement in the shaky business of judging is essential to the play; and it depends on precisely that uncertainty about the characters which so often frustrates us. We know of Hamlet's or Edgar's designs because they tell us about them. We know when Iago is feigning honesty or Macbeth loyal hospitality; we know precisely to what degree we can rely upon Claudius's or Gloucester's or Othello's or Duncan's judgment of the situation. But we do not always know when Antony and Cleopatra are feigning; and it is essential that we should not know. In order to be engaged in the movement of judgments, in order to see both the validity and the limitations of all perspectives, we must be able to accept each of the various judgments as true at least momentarily. To do so we cannot know substantially more about the protagonists than the characters who judge them know. And it is this movement of perspectives, rather than the revelations of a psychodrama or the certainties of a morality, which is most characteristic of *Antony and Cleopatra*.

The uncertainty of judgment characteristic of *Antony and Cleopatra* depends on our ignorance of the inner states of the characters and on their own insistent questioning; but it is also built into the dramatic structure of the play. In one sense, the experience of *Antony and Cleopatra* is curiously indirect: the play consists of a few actions and almost endless discussion of them. Antony is the presumptive hero of the play; when he appears in act 2, scene 2, he has been absent for three scenes during which Caesar, Cleopatra, and Pompey have in their speculations created three distinct Antonys, each to their heart's desire. Which Antony do we know? We never actually see Cleopatra in mythological garb, yet she is twice described in the habiliments of a goddess: Enobarbus reports her appearance as Venus, and Caesar her appearance as Isis. These two reports are strikingly different in attitude; the difference between them suggests two possible perspectives on Cleopatra, and on the quasidivinity sometimes associated with her, far more economically than any dramatic action could. We do not see Antony's return to Egypt: we learn of it only as Octavia does, from the not impartial report of her brother. This insistence upon report and discussion makes us suspect that the actions are unimportant except insofar as they are interpreted; in fact, the dramatic design of *Antony and Cleopatra* forces us to acknowledge the process of judgment at every turn. When the audience is persistently told one thing and shown another or told two conflicting things, when it sees minor characters speculating about the protagonists almost as often as it sees the protagonists themselves, then its own process of judgment becomes part of the experience of the play. It is the very indirectness of *Antony and Cleopatra* that insures the direct participation of the audience in it.

The most characteristic dramatic technique in *Antony and Cleopatra* is the discussion of one group of characters by another. In its purest form, it is strikingly simple: a group of minor characters who are alone on stage discuss an action that is about to take place among the protagonists; the protagonists then appear on stage, act, and disappear; and a group of minor characters, frequently the same as the initial group, are left to discuss the action. The scene is thus framed so that the major characters become in effect actors and the minor characters their interpretive audience. This pattern appears with astonishing consistency throughout the play. Occasionally one half of the frame is missing; but in these instances the framing effect is generally achieved by the presence of commentary on the part of the minor characters throughout whatever action is engaging the protagonists. Either partial or complete framing of this sort occurs in no less then twelve scenes; significant elements of this process occur in many more scenes. Act 1, scene 1, is the paradigm for this structural framing just as it is the paradigm for the varying perspectives of the play. Demetrius and Philo comment on the lovers; the lovers appear and simultaneously substantiate and reveal the limitations of their judges; and they are left to comment once again. Philo's language virtually forces us to see the lovers' appearance as a spectacle or a play within the play, a play with a very specific moral:

> Look, where they come:
> Take but good note, and you shall see in him
> The triple pillar of the world transform'd
> Into a strumpet's fool: behold and see.
>
> (1.1.10–13)

In act 2, scene 2, Enobarbus and Lepidus discuss the meeting of Antony and Caesar; the great triumvirs meet and the marriage with Octavia is arranged; and Enobarbus and Maecenas are left to discuss Cleopatra, Octavia, and the proposed union. The concord is a formal spectacle for which the prologue and epilogue provide the appropriate interpretation. The same pattern of formal concord and interpretive discussion is repeated in act 2, scene 6: Pompey, Antony, and Caesar meet and come to terms; Enobarbus and Menas are left to discuss the terms and to prophesy of the union between Antony and Caesar. Pompey's servants discuss the drunkenness of the world leaders before we see them in act 2, scene 7; Enobarbus and Menas stand aside and comment during part of the scene (ll. 86–94). In act 3, scene 2, Enobarbus and Agrippa discuss the farewells of Octavia, Caesar, and Antony; we then see the brothers parting while Enobarbus and Agrippa comment on their tears. Act 3, scene 7, is a variation on the pattern: Cleopatra and Enobarbus discuss the effect of Cleopatra's presence on Antony; Antony enters and apparently under Cleopatra's influence informs Canidius that he will fight by sea; Canidius and a soldier are left commenting on Cleopatra's effect on Antony and on the forthcoming battle. The most complex of these scenes is act 3, scene 13, which consists of four separate actions and Enobarbus's commentary on each of them. When the scene opens, Enobarbus and Cleopatra as prologue are discussing Antony's flaw. Antony appears and sends Caesar a challenge to single combat; Antony leaves and Enobarbus comments extensively on his folly. Next, Thidias enters and Cleopatra flirts with him; Enobarbus comments on her disloyalty to Antony. In the third section of the scene, Antony returns, oversees their dalliance, and orders Thidias punished; Enobarbus comments on his rage. Finally, after his rage, Antony is reconciled to Cleopatra and vows to do wondrous deeds in the next battle; Enobarbus comments on that diminution in his captain's brain which has restored his heart. With this final commentary, Enobarbus is again alone on stage, summarizing and judging the entire scene. But in this scene Enobarbus's asides not only function as a commentary on the main action, but become an impetus to action in themselves. In the process of commenting on Antony's folly, Enobarbus begins to judge his own ("The loyalty well held to fools does make / Our faith mere folly" [ll. 42–43]). His commentary and his consequent decision to leave Antony begin to take center stage. His death is the result of this decision; it is fitting that in his death scene the constant commentator has become the central actor upon whom others comment. In act 4, scene 9, the watchmen stand aside and comment throughout his soliloquy and after his death.

These scenes are not the critical dramatic moments in the play; they are interesting because they indicate the extent to which this pattern is habitual even in relatively peripheral scenes. And the most critical moments—Actium, Antony's suicide, and Cleopatra's suicide—all have essentially the same structure, the central action and the series of comments. In the Actium scene (3.10) the frame has in fact replaced the picture. In this scene and the one that follows, we are given a hierarchy of commentary upon a scene which takes place offstage: Enobarbus and Scarus comment; then the general Canidius comments; then, finally, Antony comments upon himself. Once the pattern has been established, it can function even when the frame appears without the picture: all those scenes in which characters discuss one another's activities serve to some extent as prologues and epilogues to actions which occur offstage. Each time the pattern occurs, it is analogous to the structure of the play as a whole—to our opaque protagonists, surrounded by critics and commentators.

By the device of partial or total framing, the structure of these scenes emphasizes the process of discussion. The effect of all this framing is to insure that we as audience will get at least as much information from the minor characters as from the protagonists. In many of Shakespeare's plays, the sources of information and their reliability are of critical importance: *Hamlet* would be a totally different experience if our principal informants throughout were Claudius or Polonius rather than the ghost and Hamlet himself. But in *Antony and Cleopatra,* information of all kinds is unreliable. The number of messengers in the play is symptomatic of this breakdown in direct and reliable communication. There are eight characters designated simply as "messenger"; to their company we must add Alexas as messenger from Antony to Cleopatra in act 1, scene 5, Menas and Varrius as news bearers to Pompey in act 2, scene 1, Antony's ambassador to Caesar in act 3, scenes 12 and 13, Thidias as Caesar's messenger to Cleopatra in act 3, scene 13, Mardian as Cleopatra's messenger to Antony in act 4, scene 14, Proculeius and Dolabella as Caesar's messengers to Cleopatra in act 5, scene 2, and the protagonists themselves when they are news bearers. Even given the military and political information which must be reported to Antony, Caesar, Pompey, and Cleopatra, the number of messengers is extraordinary. If the main function of the messengers is expository, surely Shakespeare could have found some simpler device. As it is, the audience is continually bombarded with messengers of one kind or another, not so much to convey information as to convey the sense that all information is unreliable, that it is message or rumor, not fact. In this uncertain world, even the simplest of factual messages is subject to doubt; it is no wonder that Varrius insists on the certainty of his report when he tells Pompey of Antony's whereabouts ("This is most certain, that I shall deliver" [2.1.28]). And since Shakespeare keeps us in the dark about the motivations and actions of his main characters, we as well as the characters must frequently rely upon these reports for information.

In the first scene, Antony refuses to listen to the messengers from Rome; he resolves to Cleopatra to hear "no messenger but thine" (1.1.52). When he finally listens to the two messengers from Rome and Sicyon in the next scene, their reports are unimpeachable; in the next scene, where Cleopatra tells Alexas to vary his report according to Antony's mood (1.3.2–4), we see the reliability of her messenger. But as the play progresses, reliability and unreliability are no longer so tidily apportioned between Rome and Egypt. Most of the messages in the play are in the pattern of Pompey's unsuccessful prayer: they come too late to be useful. Pompey prays that Cleopatra keep Antony in Egypt only after we know that he is on his way to Rome, thus illustrating his own maxim: "Whiles we are suitors to their throne, decays / The thing we sue for" (2.1.4–5). Immediately after we have seen Antony take his leave of Cleopatra (1.3), Caesar enters with news of Antony's revelry in Alexandria—news which is obsolete by the time we hear him speak it (1.4.3–5). Shakespeare could perfectly well have gained our full credence for Caesar's report merely by placing it one scene earlier, but instead he chooses to bewilder us: Caesar's news has been true, but we know that it is true no longer. This misalignment of report and deed is strikingly consistent in the messages which follow. Alexas presents the pearl from "the firm Roman to great Egypt" (1.5.43); when next we see the firm Roman, he is arranging his marriage with Octavia (2.2). Even the messenger who brings Cleopatra news of Antony's marriage is part of this sequence: he brings his news (2.5) only after we have heard Antony resolve to return to Egypt (2.3). Again and again, we are made aware that message and fact are askew. How does one act or judge on the basis of such information? At the end of the play, we will see the consequences of this unreliability: it is Mardian's false message from Cleopatra that causes Antony's suicide. But even Mardian's false message will be in some sense

the first Roman messenger in terms which suggest that Roman truth may not be Egyptian truth:

> Speak to me home, mince not the general tongue:
> Name Cleopatra as she is call'd in Rome;
> Rail thou in Fulvia's phrase, and taunt my faults
> With such full license, as both truth and malice
> Have power to utter.
>
> (1.2.102–6)

Both truth and malice: the truth is told, but presumably with a little warping by malice, when it is Roman truth. Octavia chides Caesar for precisely such warping:

> CAESAR. That ever I should call thee castaway!
> OCTAVIA. You have not call'd me so, nor have you cause.
>
> (3.6.40–41)

"Read not my blemishes in the world's report" (2.3.5), Antony asks Octavia: though that report may be true, it is not the whole truth. Suggestions of this flexibility of truth permeate the play:

> Who tells me true, though in his tale lie death,
> I hear him as he flatter'd.
>
> (1.2.95–96)

> They are so still,
> Or thou, the greatest soldier of the world,
> Art turn'd the greatest liar.
>
> (1.3.37–39)

> By this marriage,
>
> .   .   .   .   .   .
>
> . . .truths would be tales,
> Where now half tales be truths.
>
> (2.2.131–35)

If Enobarbus's report of Cleopatra as Venus is a half tale, is not Caesar's report of Cleopatra as Isis the sort of truth that malice would utter? At the end of the play, the Clown brings us word of the joys of the worm from "a very honest woman, but something given to lie, as a woman should not do, but in the way of honesty" (5.2.251–53). Truth and lie are bound together, as they are at the end of Chaucer's *House of Fame;* their union has already been suggested by Demetrius in the first scene of the play. We have just seen Rome's valuation of the lovers and their own valuation of themselves. The lovers leave the stage, and Demetrius says,

> I am full sorry
> That he approves the common liar, who
> Thus speaks of him at Rome.
>
> (1.1.59–61)

If the liar's speech is verified by Antony's deeds, is he nonetheless a liar? Is truth itself the common liar?

Throughout the play, the audience hears characters ask apparently unanswerable questions and watches them discuss one another without reaching any accord. We listen to a series of reports and judgments which are neither true nor false, or are both together, until even the concepts of truth and falsity lose their meanings. Shakespeare is not dallying with us only to confuse us. He is instead deliberately playing with these dramatic techniques in order to draw us into the act of judging. In effect, we are forced to judge and shown the folly of judging at the same time: our double responses are an essential part of the play. *Antony and Cleopatra* constantly insists on its status as a play: characters stage emotions and accuse one another of bad acting; the pattern of framing suggests that we see the central figures as actors in a play within the play; and Cleopatra seems to allude to one very limited interpretation of the very play that we are seeing when she fears that she will see "Some squeaking Cleopatra boy my greatness / I' the posture of a whore" (5.2.219–20). The function of all this insistence on the play as play is not merely to suggest the metaphysical proposition that all the world's a stage; it is specifically to involve us as audience in the action of the play. For we are, in a sense, the most minor of the characters who stand aside and comment; or at least we as audience are silent extensions of them.

THE VARIOUS WORLD

> *darkling stand*
> *The warying shore o' the world.*
> (4.15.10–11)

Tragedies do not normally ask us to identify ourselves with the minor characters. But in *Antony and Cleopatra* we participate in the experience of the commentators more often than in the experience of the lovers: we are forced to notice the world's view of them more often than their view of the world. There are of course moments of framing commentary in the other tragedies, moments when we are more engaged with the commentator and his perceptions than with the protagonist. Horatio in *Hamlet* and the fool in *Lear* are temporarily allowed to assert their points of view. But such moments are indeed rare; we more readily accept the protagonist's definition of himself and the world than the world's definition of him. Even in *Macbeth,* Macbeth's own sense of himself as loathsome moves us far more than the world's condemnation of him. But in *Antony and Cleopatra* the device of framing forcibly dissociates us from the lovers; their vision of themselves becomes merely one in a series of competing visions. For much of the play, we live outside their immediate universe and see them with distressing clarity from perspectives which are alien to them.

This emphasis on alien perspectives accounts, I think, for one of the structural peculiarities of the play. In most of the tragedies, virtually every event in the play is related either directly or by analogy to the tragic plot. The most common charge against the structure of *Antony and Cleopatra* is that it violates this very simple structural principle: there are several distracting scenes that have nothing in particular to do with the tragic plot, that is, with the downfall of the lovers. Even the play's staunchest supporters often find themselves embarrassed by such apparent excrescences as the Ventidius scene (3.1). We cannot blame this apparent structural laxity on the unwieldy nature of the source material; for in fact Shakespeare quite ruthlessly omits everything in Plutarch's account that does not serve his purpose. We must assume, then, that Shakespeare did not give his play that concentration of structure typical of most of the tragedies for reasons of his own.

The world of *Antony and Cleopatra* is defined by violent juxtapositions and contrasts. The most powerful of these contrasts are unavailable to the reader in his study; they are made in purely theatrical terms, through what Charney calls "presentational imagery." In act 1, scene 5, we see Cleopatra lounging among her attendants, imagining Antony's soldiership and recalling Caesar and great Pompey, who "would stand and make his eyes grow in my brow" (l. 32). There is an absolute indolence about the scene, as though we have all drunk mandragora to sleep out the great gap of time. The next scene must follow immediately upon this one (it is only through the accidents of editorial scene division that it does not); it presents the sharpest possible dramatic contrast. *"Enter Pompey, Menecrates, and Menas, in warlike manner"*

(2.1). Everything about this scene is as upright and energetic as the previous scene was indolent; here we see warfare in good earnest, not the version which Cleopatra chooses to imagine or recall. This scene is by no means necessary to the plot; we do not need to see Pompey in his camp. He serves merely to necessitate the temporary union of Antony and Octavius; a report of his sea power would accomplish the same end. In fact he is so superfluous a character that Shakespeare kills him off in a subordinate clause: Antony "threats the throat of that his officer / That murder'd Pompey" (3.5.18–19). Even the fate of poor Lepidus receives more extended treatment. But we do see Pompey in his own camp; we do see from his perspective, however momentarily. Precisely the same sort of theatrical contrast is made when Ventidius enters in triumph; again the scene has been separated from its complement by editorial whim. In act 2, scene 7, we see the world leaders drunk, reclining or dancing; they leave the stage and suddenly *"Enter Ventidius as it were in triumph . . . the dead body of Pacorus borne before him"* (3.1). As in the Pompey scene, the contrast is made explicit in the stage direction. Moreover, we have just heard the treacherous Menas address Enobarbus as "noble captain" in the last line of act 2, scene 7; five lines later, Ventidius is addressed as "noble": the echo should emphasize the theatrical point. Again the scene is unnecessary for the plot; again it provides us with a radically disjunctive perspective.

In the earlier tragedies, we are not given perspectives which are totally unrelated to those of the protagonists; in *Antony and Cleopatra,* we are. We expect to see Caesar at Actium as we expect Malcolm at Dunsinane, but we do not expect to see Pompey at the Mount; it is rather as though we were to pay a momentary visit to Fortinbras before he left Norway or to the captain of the Turkish fleet in *Othello.* To clarify this distinction, let us look for a moment at two scenes: the appearance of Fortinbras in *Hamlet* (4.4) and the appearance of Ventidius here. These scenes are superficially similar: both function fundamentally to contrast a strong and decisive man of action, an efficient soldier, with the protagonist; both are interpolated into the main action and apparently unrelated to it. But it is precisely the similarity in the two scenes of martial activity that allows us to see their fundamental difference. However surprised we are by Fortinbras's appearance in *Hamlet,* he does reappear at the end of the play as a figure of some consequence. Moreover, Hamlet himself speaks with one of Fortinbras's captains; we are essentially aware of Hamlet's responses in this scene. Fortinbras's appearance is the occasion for a soliloquy; the hero not

only watches the action but explicitly comments on the contrast between Fortinbras and himself. But what of Ventidius? He appears on
the outer edges of the empire; none of the protagonists witnesses his
appearance. They never discuss him in the course of the play, though
he discusses them. And while his bearing serves as a contrast to the
bearing of the drunken world leaders on Pompey's galley and his fear
of carrying the battle further serves to indicate the effects of triumviral
degeneracy on subordinate officers, he is related to the protagonists
only in the most tenuous way; he cannot in any sense be said to
explicate Antony's condition as Fortinbras explicates Hamlet's. Both
the Pompey and the Ventidius scenes present a radical contrast to the
perspective of the protagonists; and it is precisely in forcing us to move
from one perspective to the next abruptly and without mediation that
Antony and Cleopatra achieves its most characteristic effects. Such
unanticipated shifts in perspective force upon us an awareness of *scope*,
of how various a place the world is.

In the other tragedies, even the most minor of the characters tend
to take part in the one great tragic event. The musicians in *Othello* give
us an image, however imperfect, of that harmony which Iago will
successfully untune. Macbeth's devil-porter identifies his castle as a
kind of hell, in case we were in danger of forgetting; and Macbeth is of
course his master-devil. The gravedigger in *Hamlet* represents a point
of view strikingly different from that of the over-curious prince; but he
introduces us to Ophelia's maimed rites and moreover serves as a
significant teacher in Hamlet's education to accept mortality. But what
of similar scenes in *Antony and Cleopatra*? The serving men on Pompey's
galley do not reflect Antony's condition, nor are they involved in any
way in his action. When Lepidus, Maecenas, and Agrippa arrange to
meet at Mount Mesena (2.4), they scarcely mention the protagonists;
nor is the farewell of these subordinates in any way significant to the
protagonists. The varied personages in *Antony and Cleopatra* come
forth, posit their own diverse points of view, and then disappear; they
remain autonomous and insist that we notice the multiplicity of this
world.

This insistence on the varying shores of the world is not common
in Shakespearean tragedy. In the major tragedies, the presentation of
character and the structure generally function to focus our attention on
the protagonists, to force us to participate in their experience and to
live for a time within the moral contours of their universe. To participate fully in the tragic experience, we must be willing, for the mo-

ment, to see the universe through the eyes of the protagonist and entirely in relation to him: we must experience Lear's storm as he himself experiences it. This concentration of vision allows us to perceive the sufferings of Edgar and the fool on the heath as fragmentary versions of Lear's suffering; it allows us to feel that Gloucester's blinding is part of Lear's experience even before Lear is aware of it. In order to achieve this concentration of vision, we must be given some knowledge of the inner state of the protagonist; we must be allowed to see how he perceives the world before we can participate in his perceptions. Lear on the heath conducts a virtually continuous soliloquy, whether other characters overhear him or not; Hamlet, Othello, and Macbeth constantly tell us how the world seems to them. But this kind of knowledge is usually denied us in *Antony and Cleopatra;* and the dramatic structure functions to diffuse and dissipate our attention throughout a wider universe than that which the protagonists know. We expect to see the universe only insofar as it reflects the experience of the protagonists; but we see the universe as prior to and independent of them.

It is of course true of all the tragedies that the audience sees a more varied world than the protagonists; we never share their vision entirely. But in the other tragedies, the exclusiveness of the protagonist's vision and our partial absorption into it are essential to the tragic effect. Their vision becomes progressively narrowed until fewer and fewer possibilities are left open to them: Lear's world contracts until it does not include the possibility of kindly daughters, Othello's the possibility of Desdemona's innocence; Macbeth gradually loses sight of any world outside his own diseased fantasy. In these plays, the audience participates both in the narrowing of vision and in an awareness of what is excluded; we share in the constriction although we see the protagonist trapped by it. *Othello* is horrifying partly because we are made to experience Othello's abused perception even while we know it is wrong; for most of *Macbeth,* our experience is as claustrophobic as Macbeth's. When we are finally given sight of King Edward's or Cordelia's healing nature, our relief is enormous precisely because we too have been trapped by the protagonist's vision. Part of the effect of these plays depends on our ability to see through the protagonist's eyes, even when we see possibilities unacknowledged by him. But this progressive narrowing and widening of our vision is foreign to *Antony and Cleopatra*: there the exclusivity of the protagonists' vision never becomes part of our experience; we are given competing visions throughout.

Multiplicity of all kinds is essential to the structure of *Antony and Cleopatra*: throughout most of the play the world is an enormously crowded place. This multiplicity is achieved not only through the introduction of apparently unrelated characters and scenes but also through a structural principle of varied repetition, rather like a musical theme and variations. The audience continually sees the same actions, hears the same metaphors, but always with a slight variation; and this structural repetition suggests widely varying versions of experience just as the framing commentary suggests varieties of judgment. We are given, for instance, a series of servants who desert their masters and masters who desert their servants, each of whom comments by implication on the rest. Shortly after Enobarbus has announced that he will "seek / Some way to leave" Antony (3.13.200–201), Antony himself addresses his servants "as one that takes his leave" (4.2.29): Enobarbus weeps over Antony's leave-taking even as he plans his own. In the next scene, we hear that "the god Hercules, whom Antony lov'd, / Now leaves him" (4.3.15–16). This action reiterates the central action of Actium, in which Antony quite literally leaves his servants; and it complements the action of all those servants who leave their masters throughout the play. Menas deserts Pompey because Pompey is not sufficiently ruthless to deserve service; Alexas and Canidius and the rest desert Antony because Antony has deserted his followers and in some sense himself at Actium; Enobarbus deserts Antony because it appears to him that Cleopatra and his own discretion have deserted Antony. Seleucus deserts Cleopatra for reasons that remain obscure: if his betrayal is not staged (and there is no real reason to assume that it is), then his behavior is, at the least, ungenerous. Dolabella temporarily deserts Octavius for love of Cleopatra; his betrayal of his master's plans is one of the few moments of compassion at the end of the play. Decretas deserts Antony, presumably because dead masters are not profitable to work for; but his eulogy of Antony reminds us that he knows his master's worth and is willing to assert it even to Caesar. If Decretas complicates the pattern of betrayal, Scarus reverses it altogether. He too seems inclined to desert Antony after Actium (3.10.32–33), but in the proof, he is magnificently loyal. Enobarbus dies of a broken heart because he has deserted Antony. Eros kills himself to avoid obeying his master's command; his magnificent disobedience may be seen as a commentary on the disobedience of all the unreliable servants in the play. Antony has previously deserted Fulvia, Octavia, and Cleopatra; Cleopatra seems momentarily to regard his death as a desertion ("Noblest of men, woo't die? / Hast thou no care of me?" 4.15.59–60). Servants and masters desert, in short, with every reason and under every circumstance; the pattern is repeated with endless variation. Our impression is simultaneously that nothing changes and that nothing is the same.

The same sense of endless likeness and endless difference is achieved by this kind of repetition throughout the play: in the reception of bad news, for instance, or in the repeated episodes of handshaking or hand kissing. After Actium, Scarus tells us that Antony has "kiss'd away / Kingdoms, and provinces" (3.10.7–8); Antony himself kisses Cleopatra and says, "Even this repays me" (3.11.71). Cleopatra wishes that her kiss could quicken the dying Antony (4.15.39), but her kiss kills Iras (5.2.292). Has she the aspic in her lips? We are given both Charmian's figs (1.2.32) and the figs that bring death to Cleopatra and her maidens; the reverberations set up between the first fig and the last suggest a whole complex of attitudes toward life and its pleasures. Decretas's theft of Antony's sword would not be so shocking if we had not seen Eros practice a different swordplay only a few moments before. Eros draws his own sword to kill himself for love of Antony; Decretas steals Antony's sword to make matters right with Caesar. The contrast could scarcely be more sharply drawn than by the repeated use of the sword. The three images of entrapment in the play suggest the variety of perspectives with extraordinary economy. Cleopatra decides to go fishing and imagines each fish an Antony (2.5.11–14); she obviously thinks of herself as an amiable trap. But there is nothing amiable about the image of the trap when she greets Antony after his victory: "com'st thou smiling from / The world's great snare uncaught?" (4.8.17–18). Cleopatra as snare or the world as snare? Which finally captures Antony? Caesar complicates the image further: Cleopatra looks "as she would catch another Antony / In her strong toil of grace" (5.2.345–46). For him, Cleopatra is clearly the snare; nonetheless, there are presumably worse fates than being caught in a toil of *grace*.

The achievement of simultaneous perspectives through varied repetition works throughout the play. When we hear the music of Hercules departing, we are reminded of a thematic pattern of enormous complexity. The music of the departing god is the first we know of his presence; we recognize the supernatural only as it withdraws. This pattern of the presence known too late is a variation of the "She's good, being gone" (1.2.123) theme initiated by Antony's reaction to Fulvia's death and repeated whenever we see someone weep what willingly he did confound; it anticipates such critical moments as Enobarbus's discovery of Antony's full generosity only after he has deserted him, Antony's reaction to the report of Cleopatra's death, and Cleopatra's deification of Antony after his death. Cleopatra's dream of her emperor and the political tears which Octavius sheds for Antony are variations on the same theme. The function of varied repetition is most striking in the association of love, war, and death, an association posited by widely differing characters with widely differing perspectives. For Philo and Pompey, the association represents the misapplication of a soldier's talents (1.1.6–10; 2.1.12–13). Agrippa is more amused than appalled by the association: "She made great Caesar lay his sword to bed" (2.2.227). The death of the character named Eros, with his sword drawn, is the objectification of the association on stage; in his death, the comic perspective is transformed utterly. Enobarbus's comment on Cleopatra's "celerity in dying" (1.2.142) will be similarly transformed when Caesar tells us of Cleopatra's pursuit of easy ways to die. At their suicides, each of the lovers reiterates the association of love and death (4.14.99–101; 5.2.294–95) as part of their transformation of death into reunion. But the sexual suggestiveness of the asp and the Clown's banter insure that we will not forget the other perspectives possible.

The insistence upon scope, upon the infinite variety of the world, militates against the tragic experience. We simply are not permitted the luxury of the tragic vision: our attempt to see the universe solely in terms of the protagonists in continually thwarted. For in *Antony and Cleopatra* the vision of tragedy is only part of the story. The protagonists find themselves to be of primal significance in the universe; but we must see them from other, less comfortable perspectives. We have heard of Antony's almost magical soldiership from Pompey and Caesar. In the Ventidius scene, we see it for a moment with the satiric impulse of a subordinate who works while his master plays: "I'll humbly signify what in his name, / That magical word of war, we have effected" (3.1.30–31). In Decretas, we see briefly from the point of view of a man who seems even more perfectly political than Caesar when he greets Antony's suicide with "This sword but shown to Caesar with this tidings, / Shall enter me with him" (4.14.112–13); but we also see him deliver a potentially dangerous eulogy of Antony to Caesar. The dramatic contrasts and the varied repetitions insist that we move among several versions of experience, among the comic and satiric as well as the tragic.

COMIC PERSPECTIVES

If you find him sad,
Say I am dancing.
(1.3.3–4)

The uncertainty and variety characteristic of *Antony and Cleopatra* frequently militate against its tragic effect. But if the play is not simply a defective tragedy, then what is it? In most tragedies, the protagonists confide in the audience; we can usually take the tragic hero as seriously as he takes himself. But in *Antony and Cleopatra* we see through the eyes of the commentators more often than through the eyes of the protagonists; and the commentators seldom take the protagonists as seriously as they might wish. In fact, a dramatic structure in which the minor characters continually intervene between the protagonists and the audience is more characteristic of farce than it is of tragedy: at moments, *Antony and Cleopatra* is closer to Plautine comedy than to *Hamlet*. Take, for instance, the long scene in which Antony's challenges to Caesar, his rage against Thidias, and his renewed promises of derring-do are punctuated by Enobarbus's caustic asides. The relation of actor to commentator in this scene has a venerable ancestry in the tradition of the *miles gloriosus*: Antony boasts and rages like the braggart soldier; Enobarbus undercuts him like the tricksy slave. Maynard Mack has pointed out that these "paired voices" occur in all the tragedies. But in the other plays, the heroic voice is, I think, strengthened by the presence of the opposing voice; in *Antony and Cleopatra,* our allegiance is more often divided. There are surely moments of a tragic involvement with the protagonists; but there are also moments of a comic detachment.

The very process of varying perspectives is essentially a comic technique. In tragedy, everything usually tends to confirm the experience of the tragic hero; by process of analogy even the most diverse scenes will work to substantiate his version of the world. Comedy tends, on the other hand, to work toward variety of experience, a multiplicity of versions, as tragedy does not. In *King Lear* we have a hierarchy of meaningful figures and events which have their end in the experience of Lear; in *As You Like It,* we are more interested in the juxtaposition of several contrasting figures than in any single figure. To put it, perhaps, overtidily: all the figures on the heath comment on Lear's experience in a way that all the figures in the Forest of Arden simply do not comment on the duke's or Rosalind's or Orlando's. We think of all the versions of love which exist simultaneously in the Forest of Arden; and though we find Rosalind's the least constricting, our experience of the play depends not solely on her version but on the simultaneous perception of them all. Juxtaposition of this sort is of course essential to the structure of plays like *Midsummer Night's Dream, As You Like It, Twelfth Night,* and, to a lesser degree, *The Tempest;* and it is foreign to the structure of the tragedies. Simultaneous versions of experience which can compete on equal footing are generally not given us in the tragedies; in *Antony and Cleopatra,* we are given precisely this simultaneity of competing versions.

I am of course oversimplifying this distinction; *Antony and Cleopatra* has more in common with *King Lear* than with *Midsummer Night's Dream.* But there is a surprising prevalence of essentially comic technique in the structure of *Antony and Cleopatra;* and to regard these comic techniques as surface excrescences on a fundamentally tragic play is surely as serious an error as to overemphasize them. There are comic elements in other tragedies: Othello, like Antony, is a type of the *miles gloriosus.* But in *Othello,* this comic structure is transformed to serve a tragic purpose: the tragedy consists precisely in the relationship between him and his tricksy servant. Generally, comic elements in the other tragedies are subsumed into the tragic vision as they are not in *Antony and Cleopatra.* For the comic moments in this play—such moments as Charmian's baiting Cleopatra about her love for Caesar—are not isolated phenomena: the entire tragic vision of the play is subjected to the comic perspective. If this double perspective is perilous to the structure of the play as tragedy, it is nonetheless its peculiar triumph. It is the unique excellence of *Antony and Cleopatra* that it does not allow us to maintain the comfortable and certain attitudes of either comedy or tragedy for very long. We are not permitted the luxury of total engagement with the protagonists; nor are we permitted the emotional safety of total detachment from them. We think we know where we stand; and then we feel the ground shifting under our feet. To restrict the play solely to either the tragic or the comic perspective is to make it a much safer play than it actually is: there is always safety for an audience in certainty, even if the certainty is as painful as it usually is in Shakespearean tragedy. But we do not know how to regard *Antony and Cleopatra*: for the play is essentially a tragic experience embedded in a comic structure. In that sense it is as treacherous and painful as life itself: each of us has moments in which we experience our lives with a tragic concentration and intensity; but each of us must know that these

"Nature's Piece 'Gainst Fancy": The Divided Catastrophe in *Antony and Cleopatra*

Anne Barton

When Ajax, in Sophocles' play, announces that from now on he will humble himself before heaven, that he is going down to the sea to cleanse himself of blood and to bury Hector's unlucky sword, it seems for a moment that there will be no tragedy. The hero's words, however, were double-edged. When he reaches the sea, Ajax buries the sword of Hector in his own heart. Abruptly, the rejoicings of the Chorus turn to lamentation. Tecmessa discovers and shrouds her husband's body. Ajax's brother Teucer points bitterly to the ineluctable nature of divine will. The tragic movement of the play appears, at this point, to have completed itself. We have lived through a reversal and a discovery and, whatever Aristotle really meant by *catharsis*, it seems that we have had the experience or something like it: have participated in and been changed by pity and fear. It seems positively perverse that Sophocles should not only extend his tragedy beyond this climactic moment, but extend it for almost four hundred lines. Why, when he could have ended with Ajax's heroic death and the valedictions of Teucer and the Chorus did he insist upon a long, unpredictable final movement occupied entirely by the struggle between Teucer, Menelaus, Agamemnon and Odysseus over the issue of whether Ajax's body should be buried properly, or simply left above ground to rot?

Some very unkind things have been said over the years about the construction of Sophocles' *Ajax*. Indeed, "broken-backed" is a com-

From *An Inaugural Lecture* (to the Hildred Carlile Chair of English Literature in the University of London tenable at Bedford College, October 1972). © 1973 by Anne Barton.

ment that can still be heard. The trouble is that Sophocles seems to have had a puzzling predilection for these severed spinal columns. Of the seven complete tragedies which survive, no fewer than three are "broken-backed" or, to use a term that I personally much prefer, possess a "divided catastrophe." The first three quarters of *The Women of Trachis* concerns Deianira, the neglected and ageing wife of Heracles. When her son tells her that the "love-charm" she sent to her husband has destroyed him, she says farewell to the household things which symbolised her marriage, and then kills herself with a sword. Her body is displayed to the horrified Chorus of Trachinian women, and an ending seems imminent. Instead, the tragedy lurches forward again as Heracles himself, a character hitherto present only in name, suddenly arrives in Trachis to die. Not only is the last movement of the tragedy wholly taken up with Heracles: it dismisses and diminishes Deianira in a way for which neither the title of the tragedy nor its previous development has left the audience prepared. Heracles is not even interested in the revelation that his wife was innocent, deceived by the centaur, and that she now is dead. She is important, to him and to everyone else, only as the agent of his fate.

On the whole, the *Antigone* has been more lavishly admired than either the *Ajax* or *The Women of Trachis*. It too, however, achieves a tragic climax and then, without warning, presses on beyond it. Antigone gives her name to the tragedy, and dominates most of it. Sophocles sends her to her death with full tragic honours. Then, almost slightingly, he forgets her to focus on Creon: a man who has appeared previously as an oppressor riding for a fall, but not really as a tragic protagonist whose annihilation could carry the whole, concluding section of the play. Sophocles even frustrates expectation by refusing to bring Antigone's body on stage at the end, to join the bodies of Creon's wife and son. It is as though he feared that, by allowing her to take her logical and natural place in this final tableau of death, he might blur the double, the essentially divided nature of the catastrophe.

No one, and most certainly not Sophocles, constructs plays in so eccentric a fashion out of carelessness or dramatic ineptitude. The risks are too obvious, the difficulty of making a divided catastrophe effective too great. It would seem more sensible to inquire into the rewards offered by a procedure so wayward, so consciously determined to defeat an audience's normal conviction that tragic action will wind itself up—as it does in Sophocles' *Oedipus Rex*—to a single, unmistakable catastrophe in which subsidiary disasters (like Jocasta's suicide) resemble the moons which circle round Jupiter: more or less simultaneous attendants, not planets in their own right. I think myself that a dramatist is likely to experiment with a divided catastrophe when he wants and needs, for some reason, to alter the way his audience has been responding to the experience of the play. Basically, it's a way of forcing reappraisal, a radical change of viewpoint just at that penultimate moment when our complacency is likely to be greatest: when we are tempted as an audience to feel superior or even dismissive because we think we understand everything.

It is important here to distinguish between the divided catastrophe and the use of the deus ex machina. When the deified Heracles descends to break the deadlock at the end of Sophocles' *Philoctetes,* when the sun-chariot comes for Medea, or Apollo forcibly prevents arson and murder at the end of Euripides' *Orestes,* we feel that the play has simply been picked up by the scruff of the neck and artificially reversed. These endings are enormously effective, but they are also ostentatiously fictional. Particularly in the hands of Euripides, the deus ex machina ending parades its own falsehood. It reminds us of the gap between the myth as it has traditionally been told and the more dispiriting and untidy but also more convincing truth of the play. A coda rather than an organic final movement, this sudden intrusion of the supernatural operates in most cases to reinforce the first, or realistic, conclusion: a conclusion expressed in terms of uresolvable human muddle and mess.

Both the deus ex machina and the divided catastrophe are ways in which dramatists can grapple with the immemorial problem of endings in fiction. Conclusions, as Frank Kermode has stated in his brilliant book *The Sense of an Ending,* are really satisfactory only when they "frankly transfigure the events in which they were immanent." Otherwise, they are likely to seem negative, an artificial absence of continuation reminding us uncomfortably that the shapeliness and pattern which art imposes upon life is unnatural anyway, and never more so than in the false finality, the arbitrarily unified focus, of most tragedy fifth acts. The deus ex machina ending deals with the problem by admitting that it is a spurious transfiguration: self-consciously fictional. The divided catastrophe operates differently. In its unpredictability, its very untidiness, it seems to reflect not the dubious symmetries of art but life as we normally experience it in a world where events invariably straggle on beyond the point that art would regard as climactic. When used with skill, the divided catastrophe achieves a genuine transfiguration of the events in which it was immanent. It imposes a new angle of vision, an alteration of emphasis which, while it need not conflict with the previous development of the tragedy, will certainly modify our understanding of that development from a point beyond it in time.

Because, for all their apparent disjunctiveness, endings of this kind rise out of, and qualify, an entire and particular dramatic complex, no two divided catastrophes are exactly alike. In the case of the *Ajax*, Sophocles obviously wanted his audience to respond fully and emotionally to Ajax himself as a great, almost superhuman figure. E. R. Dodds was at least partly right when he described this play as a unique example of a shame-culture as opposed to a guilt-culture tragedy. Ajax himself never regrets the fact that, purely out of wounded pride, he has attempted treacherously to murder all the other Greek leaders: he regrets only that, because of the intervention of Athena, he missed. So dominant is Ajax through most of the play, so engrossing and persuasive as a tragic hero, that we accept his selfishness and passionate individualism, even as we accept behaviour on the part of the heroes in *The Illiad* which, in another context, would seem outrageous. There is no rival standard, or at least there is none until the second catastrophe, when Odysseus suddenly emerges as a kind of counter-hero. The man whose behaviour in the opening moments was positively pusillanimous, who was physically terrified of approaching Ajax's tent even under the protection of Athena, stands firm now against both Agamemnon and Menelaus. Odysseus goes on insisting until he wins that the body of Ajax, his own bitterest enemy, must be honourably buried. The reasons he advances are not Teucer's, nor are they reasons that Ajax himself could have stomached, or even understood. What Odysseus sees, in effect, is that no man is an island. The predicament of being a human is common to us all, the potentiality for tragedy universal, the end the same. Ajax must be buried, whatever his sins, because (as Odysseus says) "I too shall come to that necessity." Agamemnon misinterprets this as blatant self-interest but the selfishness of Odysseus is, paradoxically, a form of generosity. Sophocles poises it against the heroic individualism of Ajax in the first catastrophe, not in order to denigrate or cancel out that catastrophe, but to modify our comprehension of it. There are other kinds of heroism, other ways of regarding the self and one's relationship to others. In the light of Odysseus's behaviour in the second catastrophe, Ajax becomes in retrospect something of a glorious anachronism: an epic hero whose attitudes we see as limited without for a moment ceasing to recognize that they were great.

Antony and Cleopatra appeared originally in the Shakespeare First Folio without act and scene divisions. This omission, as A. C. Bradley remarked, is of no particular consequence. In fact, the tragedy divides logically and inevitably into five acts. Within this overall structure, Shakespeare has created a divided catastrophe, split between acts 4 and 5. Antony's crushing defeat at Actium comes in act 3. In act 4, scenes 4 through 8, there is for him a moment of respite. Not only does he seem, momentarily, to regain his lost, heroic identity: he moves towards a reconciliation within himself of the warring values of Rome and Egypt. May it not be possible after all to be a soldier, a triumphant workman in "the royal occupation" during the day, and still return to feast and sleep with Cleopatra in the night? Scenes 7 and 8 in particular are scenes in which we delude ourselves into thinking that there will be no tragedy. Caesar is beaten back. Antony discovers that Antony can be "himself . . . but stirr'd by Cleopatra." That formula for the reconciliation of opposites which, when it appeared in the first scene of the play, so patently rang false, here becomes almost true. And, for reasons buried deep in our own psychology and in that of the play, we want terribly to believe it. After all, beneath the surface of this tragedy lies one of the great Renaissance wish-dreams: the dream not only of harmony but of exchange and union between the masculine and feminine principles.

Shakespeare's use of the Heracles/Omphale myth—Antony tricked out in Cleopatra's tires and mantles whilst she wore his sword Philippan—always seems to be regarded by the play's critics through the cold eyes of Octavius: as an indication of Antony's utter degradation. He "is not more manlike / Than Cleopatra; nor the queen of Ptolemy / More womanly than he." The indictment here seems clear-cut. The image of a transvestite Antony is not only comic in itself, it seems to epitomise the destruction of his masculinity at the hands of Cleopatra. Almost nothing in this play, however, up to the point of the final scene, is either simple or easy to judge. It is important to balance against the censure of Octavius other and more complicated Renaissance attitudes. In *Arcadia*, Sidney had treated Pyrocles' long disguise as a woman as educative, if perilous: a search for full emotional maturity. Even Artegall's shaming captivity in female dress in the castle of Spenser's Radigund was an oddly necessary part of his quest, preparation for his eventual and tempering union with Britomart, a woman who finds it natural to set out in search of her lover wearing full armour and disguised as a man. Shakespeare may or may not have been aware of the iconographical tradition of synthesis, the blurring of identity between Venus and Mars, about which Edgar Wind writes in *Pagan Mysteries in the Renaissance*. He was, however, the author of "The Phoenix and the Turtle."

The heroic Antony of past time, the one recollected by Octavius, Pompey, Philo and Demetrius, was intensely male. On one level, it is clearly bad that Cleopatra has made him womanish. On another, his Egyptian bondage asks to be read as an attempt to regain the kind of wholeness, that primal sexual unity, about which Aristophanes is half joking, half deadly serious, in Plato's *Symposium*. Certainly there is something not just unattractive but maimed about the exclusively masculine world of Rome in this play. It emerges in that distasteful all-male party on board Pompey's galley in act 2, a party which ripens towards an Alexandrian revel but never gets there, as it does in the desperately public, chilly ostentation of Caesar's affection for his sister. Octavia, it seems, is the only woman in Rome and, unlike Portia and Calpurnia, Virgilia and Volumnia, she exists only in order to be manoeuvred and pushed about by the men.

Cleopatra is as quintessentially feminine as the younger Antony was male. Left alone among women and eunuchs after Antony's departure, she finds that life is scarcely worth living. This, one would expect. And yet she does try, particularly in the second half of the play, to become a kind of epic, warrior maiden. She is not exactly cut out to be a Britomart. When she tries to act as Antony's male body-servant in act 4, she merely succeeds in putting his armour on the wrong way round. She must have looked preposterous wearing his sword. At Actium, she announces that she will appear "for a man" but, when the battle is joined, it is as a fearful woman that she runs away. Nevertheless, it is important that she should at least have tried to participate in Antony's masculine world, that he should feel that one of her rebukes to him for military delay "might have well becom'd the best of men." Like Desdemona in Cyprus, she seems for a while to reconcile opposites, to become Antony's "fair warrior."

This moment of harmony is brief. As is usual in the fourth acts of Shakespeare's tragedies, a door is left temptingly ajar to reveal the sunlit garden of a possible happy ending, and then slammed shut. What is unique about *Antony and Cleopatra* is that this door closes where it opened, in act 4, and not—as in the other tragedies—in act 5.

In scene 12 of the penultimate act, Antony loses the third and climactic battle. This time, there can be no recovery. He also loses all conviction of his own identity and all faith in his grasp of Cleopatra's let alone any belief that the values of masculine Rome and feminine Egypt might, after all, be united. Only the false report of her death can restore Cleopatra for him as a person. His own identity, from the very first scene of the play a persistent source of question and debate for the characters who surround him, now becomes for Antony himself as cloudlike and indistinct "as water is in water." For him, as for Sophocles' Ajax, the way to self-definition, to the recovery of the man that was, seems to lie through heroic suicide. Unlike Ajax, however, Antony bungles his death. The greatest soldier of the world proves to be less efficient then Eros, a former slave. Antony fails to kill himself cleanly, and no one will respond to his requests for euthanasia. Decretas simply steals his sword and carries it to Caesar in the hope of promotion. Wallowing on the ground in agony, Antony receives the equivocal news that his serpent of old Nile has once again demonstrated what Enobarbus called her remarkable "celerity in dying"—and in reviving again at a propitious moment. Because Cleopatra is too frightened to leave her monument, Antony must be hauled up to her, slowly and unceremoniously, with ropes. He finds it almost impossible to make the queen listen to his dying words, so obsessed is she with her tirade against fortune and Octavius. The advice he gives her to trust Proculeius is, characteristically, misguided. With a last attempt which, under the circumstances, seems pathetic rather than convincing, to reestablish his heroic identity as "the greatest prince o' the world . . . a Roman, by a Roman valiantly vanquish'd," he expires in his destroyer's arms.

By comparison with that of Ajax, this is not really a glorious or even a very controlled end. But it does feel distinctly like an end, in a sense that goes beyond Antony's individual death. Even at this point, this is already a long play; it positively seems to hanker after conclusion. The whole tragedy, after all, has been focussed on Antony far more than on Cleopatra. He has been the character standing, like Heracles at the cross-roads, with an important choice to make. He has done the journeying, while she stayed put in Egypt, and these journeys have not been simply geographical, but the pilgrimages of a divided mind. Rome or Egypt, virtue or vice, the active life or the life of pleasure, the Antony of the past or the sybarite of the present: these are the great antinomies between which his will has vacillated and swung and the movement has been, to a large extent, the movement of the play. Now that he is dead, the world seems almost as vacant and still as Cleopatra imagines: a "dull world, which in thy absence is / No better than a sty." There is room for tragic obsequies—"The crown o' the earth doth melt." "O, wither'd is the garland of the war"—but not, as one feels, for tragic continuation. It is true that Cleopatra remains to be accounted for, but that conclusion seems to be foregone:

> We'll bury him: and then. what's brave, what's noble,
> Let's do it after the high Roman fashion,
> And make death proud to take us. Come, away,
> This case of that huge spirit now is cold.
> Ah, women, women! come, we have no friend
> But resolution, and the briefest end.

No matter how well one knows the play, it is difficult not to be tricked at this point into believing in that "briefest end." Surely Cleopatra will send out on the spot for a commodity of asps and follow Antony without delay. What we are emphatically not prepared for is a second catastrophe sharply divided from the first: a catastrophe, moreover, which is going to occupy an entire fifth act and more than four hundred lines of the tragedy.

Historically and in Shakespeare's main source, Plutarch's life of *Marcus Antonius,* Cleopatra's death was divided from Antony's by a gap of time. I do not myself think that this is a serious consideration. Drama is an art of temporal compression. The Shakespeare who could take the liberties he did with the historical time of Hall and Holinshed in his English histories, who had already collapsed ten years of Plutarch into the playing time of *Antony and Cleopatra,* was scarcely going to worry about this piddling kind of inaccuracy. There was nothing to prevent him from doing what he had already done in *Romeo and Juliet* and *Othello:* sending the lovers to death within minutes of each other, and in the same final scene. This was the structure which Dryden adopted later in *All for Love,* where Cleopatra sinks lifeless into the arms of an Antony who has ceased to be only a short time before. Nor did Cinthio, Jodelle, Garnier and Daniel, all of whom wrote plays on the subject before Shakespeare, come any closer than Dryden to creating a divided catastrophe.

Cinthio's *Cleopatra,* published in 1583 but acted in the 1540s, opens after Actium. It concentrates on Cleopatra, although the prologue promises that some attention will be paid to Antony as well. In fact, Antony's appearances are confined to three scenes and he encounters his mistress in only one of them, the first of act 2, at which point he is already dying. The rest of the play concerns Cleopatra's preparations for her own death, preparations which cannot take long because the queen finally expires of a broken heart while conducting the funeral rites over Antony's as yet unburied corpse.

Jodelle's tragedy *Cléopatre Captive,* first presented in 1552, published in 1574, occupies itself with the last day of its heroine's life. Antonie, very recently dead, appears only at the beginning, as a singularly vindictive Senecan ghost. It seems that he is yearning for his lady's company in the underworld, not so that they may couch together on flowers or exchange reminiscences with Dido and Aeneas, but simply because he wants her to suffer hellish torment too. After this ferociously moral opening, it comes as something of a surprise to discover that Antonie's temptress is presented quite sympathetically: queenly and proud, honourable, and still deeply in love with Antonie. When, after completing her lover's obsequies, she manages to outwit Caesar and kill herself, offstage, Proculeius waxes rhapsodic about this reunion in death. Remembering the savage remarks of the ghostly Antonie, one feels that the poor queen is in for a shock.

Garnier's tragedy *Antonie* appeared in 1578 and was translated into English by the Countess of Pembroke in 1590. Like Cinthio's play, it opens after Actium, with Antonie's downfall assured, and the lovers estranged. In fact, we never see them together until the last scene, when Antonie is dead. Cléopatre, an honest and tender-hearted woman, collapses over his corpse. Apparently she has, in the politest way imaginable, willed herself to die, and done so, after completing her final couplet.

The most important of these four tragedies, from the point of view of Shakespeare's own achievement, is Samuel Daniel's closet drama *Cleopatra,* conceived as a companion piece to the Countess of Pembroke's *Antonie,* and published in 1599. Almost certainly, Shakespeare knew and was influenced by this play. A number of specific parallels between Shakespeare and Daniel, alterations or additions to the story as Plutarch told it, have been identified by Willard Farnham, Geoffrey Bullough and Kenneth Muir. It seems to have been Daniel, for instance, who suggested to Shakespeare that Cleopatra was ageing and worried about it, and also that her death scene re-created the glory of Cydnus. Of more interest to me, however, is a connection which seems to have gone unnoticed, perhaps because it is something relatively simple and verbally quite explicit in Daniel which, in Shake-speare, has not only become infinitely more complex, but also more generalised and diffuse: an underlying assumption conveyed not through direct statement but, to a large extent, through structural, visual and metaphoric means.

Daniel's Cleopatra makes a confession in her opening soliloquy which, as far as I know, is unique to this play. She states that she has been loved by so many men in her life that "I to stay on Love had never leisure." Antony was different from these other men, because he loved the autumn of her beauty: loved her indeed when she was no longer what she had been. During his lifetime, she took this love for granted, failed to distinguish it from that of a Caesar or a Pompey. Now that Antony is dead, she sees it truly and, for the first time in her life, she herself genuinely loves.

> Now I protest I do, now am I taught
> In death to love, in life that knew not how . . .
> For which in more than death, I stand thy debter,
> Which I will pay thee with so true a minde,
> (Casting up all these deepe accompts of mine)
> That both our soules, and all the world shall find
> All reckonings cleer'd, betwixt my love and thine.

This motive for suicide runs parallel through Daniel's play with Cleopatra's horror of being led in Caesar's triumph: indeed, you cannot separate them. When the Messenger enters to describe her last moments, how Honour scorning Life led forth "Bright Immortalitie in shining armour," he puns significantly on the words *part* and *touch*:

> she performes that part
> That hath so great a part of glorie wonne.
> And so receives the deadly poys'ning touch;
> That touch that tride the gold of her love, pure,
> And hath confirm'd her honour to be such,
> As must a wonder to all worlds endure.

The acting imagery here—and there is a good deal more of it in the Messenger's account—obviously caught Shakespeare's imagination. But so, I think, did Daniel's association of the poisonous touch of the asp with the touchstone that distinguishes true gold. Daniel's Cleopatra alters her attitude towards Antony after she has lost him. In her own death, she sets out to transform their story: in effect, to do the impossible, and remake past time. It is true that Daniel could not do a great deal with this idea. He was hampered, for one thing, by his obligatory French Senecanism. Shakespeare, on the other hand, did not have the Countess of Pembroke breathing down his neck, and he could exploit it fully. I think myself that his reading of Daniel's play impelled him towards the one use, in all his tragedies, of the divided catastrophe.

As a structural form, the divided catastrophe is decidedly rare in Elizabethan and Jacobean tragedy. (Its use in comedy is far more frequent, but entirely different in effect.) Ford employed it in *The Broken Heart,* when he altered what had seemed to be the settled perspective of the play, and even the meaning of its title, by pressing on beyond the deaths of Penthea and Ithocles and the sentencing of Orgilus to the unexpected and cunningly delayed love-suicide of Calantha: a princess we have been led to regard as a kind of Fortinbras or Malcolm, restoring order to the shattered state, and not as the last and, in a sense, the most important of its tragic victims. Webster, even more daringly, conducted his Duchess of Malfy to death in act 4 and then devoted a long fifth act to a demonstration of how the world—like the garden in Shelley's "The Sensitive Plant" after the death of the Lady who was its Genius—festers and becomes poisonous, good and evil tumbled together and rendered equally impotent, once she has ceased to exist. It is not only Bosola but the theatre audience which is forced into a new understanding of what the Duchess was and what she signified after the tragic climax (as it seems at the time) has already taken place.

Apart from *The Broken Heart* and *The Duchess of Malfi,* I can think of no non-Shakespearean examples of the divided catastrophe in tragedies of the period. Certainly, Cinthio, Jodelle, Garnier and Daniel avoided it in dramatising the story of Antony and Cleopatra, even as Dryden did later. All five of these plays pick up the story late in its development. They tend (Dryden excepted) to concentrate on Cleopatra at the expense of Antony, and they are very chary of showing us the lovers together. All of them dignify Cleopatra herself, for reasons that obviously have something to do with the requirements of neoclassical decorum. The trivial or discreditable features of her character as outlined by her enemy Plutarch are smoothed away. She becomes, even in Daniel, a simple and straightforward woman: a great queen, who ought to have restrained her passions, certainly, but whose loyalty to Antony is beyond question. Lies do not come easily to this Cleopatra. Garnier is the only dramatist of the five who allows her to send the false report of her death to Antony, and even he goes out of his way to excuse and explain it. When it comes to the point of her suicide, there is nothing but respect and compassion. Indeed, this response almost seems inherent in the story. Cleopatra would not, after all, seem a particularly likely candidate for inclusion in Chaucer's *Legend of Good Women,* but hers is the first story that the poet tells. He makes it clear, moreover, that she stands beside Alcetis and Philomela, Ariadne and Hypermnestra and Lucrece, solely because of the way she kept faith with Antony in her death. Even Spenser, of all people, could be grudgingly respectful of this death. Although he puts Egypt's queen in the dungeon of Lucifera's House of Pride in book 1 of *The Faerie Queene,* his description of "High-minded Cleopatra that with stroke / Of Aspes sting herselfe did stoutly kill" is at least half admiring.

As a result of their sympathetic treatment of Cleopatra, all five tragedies are to some extent morally ambiguous. Certainly, it is difficult to reconcile the attitude adopted towards her, and in particular towards her suicide, with the official commentary on the story provided by the prologues to these plays, or by those innumerable choruses of depressed Egyptians concerned to point out that the wages of lust are death, not to mention a great deal of public misery. Even Dryden, although he did without choric commentary of this kind, and rashly subtitled his play "The World Well Lost," was careful to declare in the preface that, for him, the principal appeal of the subject lay in "the excellency of the moral." It is not easy, in face of the play itself, to see just what he means.

Shakespeare, of course, greatly complicated the situation by transferring this moral ambiguity to Antony and Cleopatra themselves. As characters, they become singularly hard to assess or know. Part of their opacity springs from the fact that she has nothing even resembling a soliloquy until the last scene of the play and that Antony is not much more forthcoming about his private intentions. This reticence contrasts sharply not only with the inveterate mental unburdenings of the protagonists in Daniel or Garnier, but with Shakespeare's own, earlier tragic practice. Emrys Jones has argued, in *Scenic Form in Shakespeare,* that the construction of *Antony and Cleopatra*—the wasteful, drifting movement of all those short scenes—reflects the haphazard nature of phenomenal experience, that it seems more like the life process itself than like formal tragedy. I think that this is true, and that the effect is one that Shakespeare reinforces through his handling of the protagonists. With Romeo and Juliet before, with Othello and

Desdemona, even with Macbeth and his wife, evaluation of the two individuals concerned and of their relationship had not only been encouraged: it was possible. With Cleopatra and Antony, on the other hand, it simply cannot be managed. They are as mysterious and contradictory as people known in real life. Our place of vantage is basically that of Charmian and Enobarbus: people sufficiently close to their social superiors to witness informal and often undignified behaviour, without participating in motive and reflection like the confidantes in Garnier or Jodelle. It is true that we see more of the picture in range, if not in depth, than these attendant characters. They cannot move, as we can, from Rome to Egypt and back again within an instant, nor are they present in all the scenes. Our perspective upon the affairs of Antony and his mistress is wider than theirs, but this very breadth makes judgment more instead of less difficult.

In this tragedy, other characters are continually trying to describe Cleopatra and Antony, to fix their essential qualities in words. This impulse generates several of the great, set speeches of the play: Enobarbus's description of Cleopatra at Cydnus, or Caesar's account of Antony crossing the Alps, like a lean stag inured to privation. It also makes itself felt in less obvious ways. Because of the constant shifting of scene, the protagonists are forever being discussed by bewildered rivals or subordinates while they themselves are away in Egypt or in Rome. The results of this unremitting attempt at evaluation are bewildering. In the course of the tragedy, Antony is called "the noble Antony," the "courteous Antony," the "firm Roman," "Mars," a "mine of bounty," the "triple pillar of the world," "the demi-atlas of this earth," the "lord of lords, of infinite virtue," the "crown o' the earth," and "the garland of the war." These are only a few of the celebratory epithets. He is also "poor Antony," a "libertine," "the abstract of all faults that all men follow," a "gorgon," a "sworder," an "old ruffian," a "doting mallard," the "ne'er lust-wearied Antony" and a "strumpet's fool." There is no progression among these epithets, no sense of alteration in Antony's character during the play as there is, for instance, with Macbeth. Macbeth begins his tragedy as "worthy Macbeth" and ends it as "this dead butcher." The space between the two descriptions is that of his tragic development. Antony, on the other hand, is all the contradictory things that people say he is more or less simultaneously. Nor is there any neat division of the celebratory and the pejorative between Antony's friends and Antony's enemies. Enobarbus and Octavius are alike in acknowledging both sides of the moon: the bright as well as the dark.

Cleopatra's situation is similar. She is "great Egypt," "dearest queen," a "rare Egyptian," a "triumphant lady," "Thetis," "this great fairy," "day o' the world," "nightingale," "eastern star," a "most sovereign creature," a "lass unparallel'd"—but also a "foul Egyptian," the "false soul of Egypt," a "witch," a "gipsy," a "strumpet," a "whore," a "trull," "salt Cleopatra," a "boggler," a "morsel cold upon dead Caesar's trencher," Antony's "Egyptian dish," the "ribaudred nag of Egypt," and "a cow in June." One may begin to feel that language used so indiscriminately to describe a single personality becomes meaningless and self-defeating, that one would do better to adopt Antony's method when he described a different serpent of old Nile to the drunken Lepidus. "What maner o' thing is your crocodile?" And Antony replies:

> It is shap'd, sir, like itself, and it is as
> broad as it hath breadth: it is just so high
> as it is, and moves with its own organs. It
> lives by that which nourishes it, and the
> elements once out of it, it transmigrates.

It's of its own colour too, and the tears of it—like Cleopatra's—are wet.

The situation is made more acute by the fact that all the other characters in the play are, for Shakespeare, remarkably monolithic. Enobarbus surprises us somewhat in his death, but up to that point we are never tempted to depart from the general consensus that he is "good Enobarb," "strong Enobarb," a soldier and a blunt, honest man. Even Cleopatra can see that Octavia is "patient." For everyone else, Caesar's sister is also holy, modest, still, and a little cold. When Cleopatra, in her jealous rage, tries to add a few spurious qualities, to make out that her rival must also be dull of tongue and dwarvish, we recognise the falsehood at once—even as we do when Caesar announces smugly that he has got rid of Lepidus because Lepidus was grown too "cruel." For Caesar himself, the epithets are again consistent: "scarce-bearded Caesar," "the young man," "blossoming Caesar," "full fortuned Caesar," "the novice," the "young Roman boy." References to his youth and rising star may be made in envy or in scorn but, regardless of whether one admires it or not, there is no real ambivalence about his character.

When it comes to the vital task of assessing one another, Cleopatra and Antony seem as uncertain as everyone else. When Cleopatra learns of Antony's Roman marriage, she tries to arrive at judgment, but fails.

> Let him for ever go, let him not—Charmian,
> Though he be painted one way like a Gorgon,
> The other way's a Mars.

This Janus-faced image of Antony derives from Elizabethan perspectives: trick paintings in which the identity of the picture, the very nature of the object represented, transformed itself according to the angle from which it was viewed. Cleopatra finds that she must put up with two contradictory, but equally real images of Antony: on the one hand a Mars, "a god in love to whom I am confin'd," on the other an uncouth Gorgon with a heart of stone. Antony too wavers continually up to the point of his suicide in his estimation of Cleopatra. Is she his "most sweet queen," or a "triple-turn'd whore?" He can never be sure of her, only of his own irrational fascination, and even that has its ebbs and flows. He loses faith again and again, mildly at the end of act 1, violently after Actium and when he catches her with Caesar's messenger in act 3, catastrophically in act 4. Cleopatra rules his life, but he remains uncertain as to just who she is. A man does not react with the hysteria of Antony at the mere sight of a messenger kissing his lady's hand unless he has hidden doubts.

We too have doubts. At the beginning of the play Antony tells Cleopatra that his love is beyond reckoning, vaster than heaven and earth. A few minutes later, he is seeking ways to break off from "this enchanting queen." What really was in his mind when he agreed so readily to marry Octavia? Is he telling the truth when he assures Caesar's sister that "I have not kept my square, but that to come / Shall all be done by the rule?" Or a moment later when he admits that "i' th' East my pleasure lies?" Cleopatra's behaviour is even more ambiguous. What was she intending to do in that scene with Thidias in act 3, when she agrees smoothly that she has never loved Antony, but merely been forced into being his paramour? Was Caesar right to think that she could be bribed to murder her lover? Again, is she betraying Caesar, or Antony, in the quarrel with Seleucus in act 5 when, after so many protestations of her intent to follow Antony in death, we find her, a boggler to the last, trying to conceal the true amount of her treasure from Octavius?

These are questions which elude resolution. Continually, the play directs one back to Cleopatra's perspective, to the monster who is also a Mars. With these two people, the same quality tends to exact contradictory descriptions, to become a vice or a virtue depending upon the position of the viewer or the particular moment of time. So, Cleopatra's infinite variety, the thing which holds Antony captive in Egypt for so long, both is and is not the same as her regrettable propensity to tell lies. Enobarbus himself, that shrewd and cynical commentator, cannot distinguish between her charm and her deceit at a number of crucial moments in the play. Nor, alas, can he separate Antony's extravagance, that culpable waste about which Caesar is so censorious, from Antony's bounty: the godlike generosity of spirit which makes Antony send Enobarbus's treasure after him when he defects to Caesar, and breaks the soldier's heart. Antony's behaviour, as Philo complains in the opening scene, "o'erflows the measure," but the very phrase reminds us that when the Nile does exactly this it showers largesse and prosperity on everyone around. Caesar's "bounty," on the one occasion when the word is associated with him, in the second scene of act 5, is a meaningless abstraction: a political lie invented by Proculeius in the hope of deceiving Cleopatra. Antony's "bounty" is not like this. A protean and mercurial thing, it is as stunning and unnecessary as the spontaneous leaps of the dolphin, and as difficult to order or assess. The worst things about Cleopatra and her lover are also, maddeningly, the best.

Like the vagabond flag of Caesar's image, *Antony and Cleopatra* up to the point of its final scene, "goes to and back, lackeying the varying tide, / To rot itself with motion." This restlessness is expressed not only in terms of a continual shifting of place, from Alexandria to Rome, to Misenum, to Athens, to Parthia, to Rome again, to Egypt, but also of the vacillation of the perspective picture, Mars dissolving into the Gorgon and then again becoming Mars. By the end of act 4, we long for stasis, for the movement to stop. But it does not. Most of act 5 is taken up with Cleopatra's hesitation and delay. Indeed, all of its dramatic tension derives from our uncertainty as to whether, despite all her protestations, she will keep her word and follow Antony in death. And, oddly enough, in a way for which there is no parallel in any other Shakespearean tragedy, we want Cleopatra to die. The reaction is one that flies in the face of normal tragic convention. After all, most of the suspense generated in the fifth act of *Hamlet* springs from our hope that somehow Hamlet himself will manage both to kill Claudius and to escape alive. In *Othello*, there remains the tantalizing possibility that the Moor will see through Iago and recognize Desdemona's innocence before it is too late, or, in *Romeo and Juliet,* that Juliet will wake before Romeo takes the poison. Only in *Antony and Cleopatra* do we long for a protagonist who has not, like Macbeth, been a villain to decide to die and do so.

Shakespeare's reason for employing the double catastrophe was, I think, precisely to elicit this unconventional reaction from the audience, and then, to gratify our desires in a way that modifies our feelings about the entire previous development of the tragedy. As Cleopatra wavers and procrastinates, we see that there can be only one way of putting doubt and ambiguity to rest. This love story has hovered continually between the sublime and the ridiculous, the tragic and the comic. We have never been able to decide which of the two sets of perspective images was the right one, or to reach any compromise between them. Only if Cleopatra keeps faith with Antony now and dies can the flux of the play be stilled and their love claim value. The act itself is indeed one that "shackles accident and bolts up change," and not merely in the sense that it will free Cleopatra herself from mutability and time. It will also transform the past, remake it in terms more far-reaching than anything envisaged by Daniel's Cleopatra. The vagabond flag will come to rest, leaving the triple-turned whore a lass unparallel'd, the Gorgon an immutable if injudicious Mars. It may even be possible to adumbrate a reconciliation between masculine Rome and feminine Egypt more lasting than the one achieved so briefly in act 4: one which will diminish Caesar forever as half-human by comparison.

Caesar, of course, is the enemy. He wants passionately to get a living Cleopatra back to Italy because, as he says, "her life in Rome / Would be eternal in our triumph." If only he can do this, he will fix the qualities of the story forever in his own terms, which are those of the strumpet and the gorgon, not the lass unparallel'd and the Mars. Cleopatra will fade into a mere parody queen in the epic pageant of his own imperial greatness, and Antony become the brother-in-arms who deserted his superior for a light woman and got what he deserved. This threat makes it imperative not only that Cleopatra should die, but that she should die in the way she does: ostentatiously as a tragedy queen. Shakespeare makes us understand that the achievement was difficult. Cleopatra at last makes up her mind. Despite her apparent duplicity with Seleucus, her anxious enquiries as to Caesar's intentions, and her own fear of physical pain, she does finally recognise and repudiate Octavius's plan: "He words me, girls, he words me, that I

should not be noble to myself." She understands what will happen in
Rome:

> the quick comedians
> Extemporally will stage us, and present
> Our Alexandrian revels; Antony
> Shall be brought drunken forth, and I shall see
> Some squeaking Cleopatra boy my greatness
> I' th' posture of a whore.

If she does not die well, this is the way her story, and Antony's, will be
told for all of time that matters. The puppeteers, the ballad-makers and
the quick comedians will cheapen and impoverish a love which was
flawed at best, but never just absurd.

Appropriately, the last obstacle Cleopatra faces on her way to
death is Comedy: personified by that ribald and garrulous countryman
who brings her asps concealed in his basket of figs. Patiently, she
listens and even responds to the clown's slanders about women, to a
kind of sexual innuendo that threatens to diminish the whole basis of
love tragedy. When he cautions her that the worm is not worth
feeding, she asks humorously: "Will it eat me?" and one realises that
she has brought together and reconciled in death two warring images
of herself from earlier in the play: the positive one in which she was "a
morsel for a monarch," but also Antony's savage description of her as
mere broken meats: "a morsel cold upon dead Caesar's trencher."
When she finally persuades the clown to depart—and the woman
committed to tragedy has to ask comedy to leave no fewer than four
times—we feel that precisely because she has walked through the fire
of ridicule, the thing she most dreads and potentially the thing most
deadly for her, she has earned the right to say, "Give me my robe, put
on my crown, I have / Immortal longings in me." And she does so at
once, without a break or a mediating pause. Comedy simply flowers
into tragedy.

"Immortal," of course, was one of the words that the clown
stumbled over most comically: "I would not be the party that should
desire you to touch [the worm]," he cautioned, "for his biting is
immortal: those that do die of it, do seldom or never recover." It must
have taken courage for Cleopatra to use that word "immortal" again,
so differently, within so short a space of time. She succeeds, however,
in winning it back as part of the vocabulary of tragedy. Indeed, she
even imposes, in retrospect, a truth upon the clown's blunder that he

never intended: the biting of this particular asp will indeed be "immortal," the agent of Cleopatra's, and through her of Antony's, undying fame.

Cleopatra dies perfectly, as a tragedy queen. In doing so, she not only redeems the bungled and clumsy nature of Antony's death in act 4 by catching it up and transforming it within her own, flawless farewell; she crystallises and stills all the earlier and more ambiguous tableaux of the play—Cydnus, her appearance throned in gold as the goddess Isis, even the dubious spectacle presented to the Roman messenger in the opening scene. This is a divided catastrophe of a very special kind. Not only does it alter the way we feel about the previous development of the tragedy, hushing our doubts about Cleopatra's faith, it makes us understand something about historical process. After all, there does seem to have been something about Cleopatra's death as the story was perpetuated in time that made it impossible for Cinthio and Jodelle, Garnier and Daniel, not to mention Chaucer and Spenser, to condemn her, whatever the overall moral pattern of the poem or play in which she appeared. There are no satirical comedies about Antony's infatuation with an Egyptian whore.

Shakespeare's second catastrophe stands as a kind of explanation of this phenomenon. Cleopatra's death, as he presents it, demonstrates how the ending of this story transfigured its earlier, more suspect stages. The modification of feeling which it imposes upon us as an audience is a repetition and reenactment of what has happened within historical time. In the play itself, we watch as Octavius acquiesces to Cleopatra's tragedy, consents (indeed) to become its Fortinbras. Here will be no parody queen led in triumph before a hooting mob, no bawdy Roman ballads, no comic puppet-shows presenting and coarsening the revels of Alexandria. Instead,

> She shall be buried by her Antony.
> No grave upon the earth shall clip in it
> A pair so famous . . . . Our army shall
> In solemn show attend this funeral,
> And then to Rome. Come, Dolabella, see
> High order in this great solemnity.

Because Cleopatra has left him no real choice, Caesar consents to become an actor in her tragedy. Indeed, his order that the Roman army should, "in solemn show," attend her funeral merely extends and develops Cleopatra's final pose.

Does it diminish Cleopatra in our eyes that the last scene of her life was just that: a tragic pose? That she assumes costume and a role, gathers Iras and Charmian as minor players around her, ransacks the treasuries of rhetoric, and confronts Caesar and his soldiers when they break in upon her with a contrived and formal tableau of death which they understand as such? I think not. When he remembered Cleopatra at Cydnus, Enobarbus said that the sight "beggar'd all description." As she lay in her pavilion, she o'er-pictured "that Venus where we see / The fancy outwork nature." That is, the living Cleopatra surpassed a picture of Venus in which art itself had outdone reality. Cleopatra herself develops this favorite Renaissance paradox when she tells Dolabella, shortly before her death, about the mythical Antony of her dreams: "His legs bestrid the ocean, his rear'd arm / Crested the world: his voice was propertied / As all the tuned spheres." Asked if there "was or might be such a man / As this I dreamt of," Dolabella answers literally: "Gentle madam, no." And Cleopatra flashes out:

> You lie up to the hearing of the gods.
> But if there be, or ever were one such,
> Its past the size of dreaming: nature wants stuff
> To vie strange forms with fancy, yet to imagine
> An Antony were nature's piece 'gainst fancy,
> Condemning shadows quite.

An Elizabethan cliché, the conceit of an art more realistic than reality itself, acquires in the second catastrophe of *Antony and Cleopatra* a very special meaning. Cleopatra here bestows upon Antony an heroic identity so colossal, but also in a sense so true—after all, those kingdoms dropping like plates, unregarded, from his pockets summon up the careless Antony we have always known—that it will defeat Time. She is also working towards her own death scene, a fictional masterpiece of another kind which is going to outclass the normal fictions of tragedy by also being real. In this death, reality will borrow the techniques of art as a means of fighting back against oblivion. Moreover, it will be victorious. Hitherto, all the images of stasis offered by a tragedy yearning towards rest have been either distasteful, like Caesar himself and his "universal peace" spread through a silent world from which everything remarkable has departed, or else obviously fragile: "the swan's down feather, / That stands upon the swell at the full of tide, / And neither way inclines." We know that, in the next moment, the tide will ebb. It is Cleopatra who finally arrests the eddying of the vagabond flag, who gives to the swan's down feather an immutable poise. She does so by creating a tableau, "still and contemplative in living art," which transfigures and quiets the events in which it was immanent in a way that Sophocles, surely, would have understood.

The Significance of Style

Rosalie L. Colie

In *Antony and Cleopatra*, the problem of style, although equally telling, is set entirely differently [than in *Julius Caesar* and *Coriolanus*]. Oratory and public speaking are not at issue in this play, are not the plot-elements they are in both *Julius Caesar* and *Coriolanus*. Nor is style displayed at the outer surface of the play, as in *Love's Labour's Lost* styles are animated into personality. Nonetheless, its peculiar language is a major force in the play, as critics from Dr. Johnson to Maurice Charney have pointed out; in comparison to the plainer speech of the other Roman plays, the verbal richness of *Antony and Cleopatra* demands attention not only for its spectacular imagery but also as a function of the play's subject. As in *Julius Caesar*, where the economical style seems properly mated to its severe subject, so in *Antony and Cleopatra* the abundance of the language seems to match the richness of its subject, the fertility of the Egyptian setting, the emotional largesse of hero and heroine. The play's language bursts with energy and vigor; figures abound; of figures, as Charney so cleverly shows, hyperbole is particularly common, that overreacher of the figures of speech. Indeed, the figures are so numerous and so rich that at times they seem almost to crowd out other meanings, to stop the action and the plot, to force attention to their resonances alone. Enobarbus's speech on Cleopatra is one example, the most famous of the play's set-pieces; Cleopatra's memories of the absent Antony, her paean to Dolabella, Antony's evaluations of his own emotional and worldly situations raise speech above the movement of plot.

From *Shakespeare's Living Art.* © 1974 by Princeton University Press.

Magniloquence fascinates both hearers and speakers. Antony's "normal" decisions to undertake his Roman responsibilities as triumvir and husband vanish in the hue and cry raised by his emotions and expressed immediately in the language he uses. More markedly, Enobarbus's famous detachment gives way before his recognition of Cleopatra's sources of power. In his great comment on her qualities his magniloquence rolls out to contrast with the plainness and irony of his previous speeches about her. In that speech, Enobarbus abandons himself to Cleopatra, and thereby gives himself away: from his response to her, apparently so out of character, we feel the force of her enchantment. Indeed, Enobarbus's giving way to grandiloquence seems an almost sexual abandon before her; the cynical and experienced Roman soldier, suspicious of Egypt and its ways, cannot and will not contain his climactic praise of the Queen.

Though the language seems at times to crowd out action and judgment, it does not crowd out meaning, for much of the meaning of this play, as one critic has argued, resides in the characters' attitudes to the language they use. The stated, plotted action of the play is in itself grand enough to require no rival in language: the range of the play is epic, over the whole Mediterranean world which was, in the Roman context, the whole world altogether. Action and scene oscillate between the poles of Rome and Egypt. From the beginning, in Philo's first speech, Rome and Egypt are set off against one another, in the shapes of Caesar and Octavia on the one side, Cleopatra on the other. The two locales, with their properly representative dramatis personae, seem to struggle for domination over Mark Antony's spirit and will. Like his great ancestor, the god Hercules, Antony stood at the crossroads of duty and sensuality, of self-denial and self-indulgence. Rome is duty, obligation, austerity, politics, warfare, and honor: Rome is public life. Egypt is comfort, pleasure, softness, seduction, sensuousness (if not sensuality also), variety, and sport: Egypt promises her children rich, languorous pleasures and satisfactions. Rome is business, Egypt is foison; Rome is warfare, Egypt is love. Egypt is "the East," where the beds are soft—and what "beds" can mean is never scanted in this play. To keep us aware of Cleopatra's power, the Romans, in their own eyes contemptuous of her life, show themselves as fascinated by Cleopatra's reputation as a bedfellow as Antony is by the actuality. Egypt is florid, decorated, deceitful, artful, opulent, sensual, idle; is "inflatus," "solutus," "tumens," "superfluens," "redundans," "enervis," "inanus." I took this list of Latin adjectives from various critiques, not of the fleshpots of Egypt, but of the Asiatic style; these epithets can, within the frame of this play, be transferred to the loose, ungirt life in Alexandria, the life to which, according to the source, Antony was inclined by temperament and which, in the end, he chooses as his own.

The question at issue is another dimension of style from those already discussed: not style as garment, or as chosen rhetoric or self-presentation, not style as manipulative instrument, but style as fundamental morality, style as life. Style of speech necessarily reveals personality, values, and ethics: one recognizes both the rectitude and the chilliness of Octavia, the silliness of Lepidus, the policy of Dolabella, from the way they speak as well as from what they say. In the speeches of Antony, Cleopatra, Octavius, Enobarbus, we recognize not just the varying moods of the speakers but their complex inner natures as well. How otherwise, indeed, could we ever assume anything about dramatic characters? Language must act to indicate quality and character, but here it does more: by reaching to the heart of the moral problems faced by Antony and Cleopatra, the language of their play makes us realize anew the ingrained connection between speech and style of life. The "square" of Roman speech and Roman life has its values, which we recognize the more easily as we see those values betrayed by Romans; the "foison" of Egypt, both its fertility and its corruption, find expression in the agon. If one felt that the play were only an essay in style as life-style, then one might draw back from it as superficial and trivial; but *Antony and Cleopatra* seems to be more than a presentation-play of theatrical and unpersoned types, more also than the psychomachia to which it is occasionally reduced. One thing that makes the play so compelling is that it *is* all these things—show, morality, exercise of power; it *is* a study in cheapness as well as in extravagance and costliness. Its chief characters are undisguisedly selfish and often trivial; in what lies its force? The language is one indicator, again, for the very style, with its grandioseness and hyperbolical explosions, finally points to the real problem: the efforts of two powerful, wilful, commanding personalities to bring their styles of living, their ingrained alien habits, into line with one another, for no reason other than love.

In a sense quite different from that of the morality-play, *Antony and Cleopatra* is about morality, about mores and ways of life—not by any means just about sexual morality, although problems of sexuality are not ignored—but about lives lived in moral terms. "Style" is—especially in the Attic-Asiatic polarity—a moral indicator, but here displayed as deeply thrust into the psychological and cultural roots of those ways of life. In this play, a given style is never merely an alternative way of expressing something: rather, styles arise from cultural sources beyond a character's choice or control.

At the beginning of the play, this does not seem to be the case: Antony doffs and dons Egyptian and Roman styles, of speech and of life, apparently at will and at need. By the play's end, he has settled for a manner of speech and behavior proved by his decisive final actions to be the signature of his inmost nature. That is to say, his style can be seen not only to express his deepest sense of self, but also to relate to the consequences of his life-choices. It is possible—indeed, it was the classical view, which Plutarch tried hard to present—to see Mark Antony's life as ruined by Cleopatra, to see the play, then, as a struggle between *virtus* and *voluptas* in which Antony fails to live up to his ancestor Hercules' example *in bivio*. But as Plutarch takes pains to tell us, and as Shakespeare in *Julius Caesar* lets us know clearly enough, there was much in Antony's temperament, bred though it was in Rome, to explain why the pull of Egypt was so strong upon him, and from Enobarbus we know how strong that pull was on anyone. Though there is a structural and thematic contrast in the play between Rome and Egypt, the scenes alternating to give us that strong sense of oscillation between these poles, the play is not so simple as a straight contest between their different values.

Seen from one perspective, Rome dominates the play: Rome's wide arch covers the epic scene, Roman policy decides the order of events and the order therefore of these important private lives. The play begins and ends with expressions of the Roman point of view; by Roman standards, Antony perishes for his failure as a Roman. But seen from another angle, Egypt commands the play, where the action begins and ends and where all the major episodes take place. In this respect, the oscillation between the two localities makes it difficult to identify a single and certain source of power. Further, the two areas are not really kept polar: Rome and Egypt interpenetrate each other, just as past history continually penetrates the play's present. Rome's impact on Egypt has helped make Cleopatra what she is; and Antony's Romanness flaws his pleasure in Egypt, even as his Egyptian experience dulls his Roman arrangements. Together and apart, Antony and Cleopatra recall their own and each other's past; Octavius speaks of Antony's and his shared past; Pompey takes the action he does because of events long over before the play begins. We see Antony unwillingly come to accept the fact that his present has been shaped by his past behavior, or that his "Rome" can never be an unqualified value again. Cleopatra dies as a Roman, or so she thinks—but does so in a décor undeniably Egyptian, and by a means particularly local. Her attributes, the iconographical details she chooses for her last tableau, are entirely Egyptian, but her suicide is itself the final Roman gesture consciously chosen.

Nor is the mixture of Rome and Egypt in her accidental: deep in her experience lay the same Julius Caesar who had such a marked effect on both Mark Antony and Octavius Caesar. Before the play's beginning, Cleopatra and her Egypt had been Romanized; by its end, she is once more Romanized, and her Egypt has finally fallen to Roman rule. Indeed, throughout the play, Egypt is constantly open to Rome: Cleopatra's relation to Julius Caesar, to Pompey, to Antony, even her efforts to charm Octavius, are symbolic of her country's dependency upon Rome's dominion. The presence at her court (a court "hers" only by the conqueror's grace) of so many Romans, full of what she calls with distaste "Roman thoughts," assures that the force of Rome upon Egypt is never unfelt, even at the height of Egyptian wassail.

However he may think of himself, Antony is a Roman soldier; Roman soldiers are always with him, even at the moment of his death. When he is away from Egypt, Roman messengers bring Cleopatra news of him and of affairs in Rome. He himself was sent to Egypt as a political administrator; he is succeeded at the play's end by Caesar himself, the last of a series of Romans proclaiming the dominion of the empire, Thidias, Dolabella, Proculeius. People die *à la romaine*: Enobarbus, Eros, Antony, Cleopatra, Charmian, Iras. Antony is borne to die his long-drawn-out death after the high Roman fashion; Cleopatra promises a like death, in which she shall be "marble constant" at the end of a life lived, publicly and privately, in significantly "infinite variety." There is no altering Roman historical destiny, however captivating Egypt and the Egyptian way of life may be.

As the play begins, we are instructed to take Roman virtues for granted as the measure from which Antony has fallen off, but as it develops, we are shown more and more to criticize in Rome. No one could be sillier than Lepidus, one of the triple pillars of the world, grosser and more clownish than any Egyptian; nor more opportunistic than Menas, whose master regrets only that Menas forced him to veto his schemes. Octavius calculates ever; Pompey seeks his own ambitious ends; Octavius's relation to Roman polity is hardly self-subordinating. Further and most important, when he is "Roman,"

Antony is at his least attractive—in his relations to his Roman wives, Fulvia and Octavia, both dismissed in his mind's economy as terms of political function. As the play advances, the notion of Rome becomes more and more tarnished, particularly in the great orgy-scene in which even Octavius's tongue "splits what it speaks," and Lepidus is carried drunk to bed (a scene unmatched in the play by the "sensual" Egyptians so constantly criticized by these same Roman tongues). In that scene, the grossness of Rome is unequivocally displayed in the unbending ambitions of Caesar, the jealousy of the triumvirs, the thinness of Pompey's honor, Menas's crude hankering after power, the heroes' dancing to their roundsong. Into such hands the world has been delivered. Of course "Egypt" offers no moral improvement over this—Cleopatra lies from first to last, to others and to herself. We are never in doubt of her duplicity, but its naturalness comes to seem worthy in comparison to the slyness of Octavius and of the "trustworthy" Proculeius. Cleopatra's is a consistent and therefore honest duplicity: her policy is innocence itself compared to the masterful and automatic deceptions of the politic Octavius. More: life in its natural spontaneity is set against machination, as Cleopatra faces Octavius symbolically and in fact. Against such an opposition, all the more obviously can Cleopatra be seen to satisfy a universal human need: though she makes hungry where most she satisfies, both hunger and satisfaction are natural enough. The Roman hunger for power can never be filled; in it there is always something barren, inhuman, and perverse—but Cleopatra can allay, even as she rekindles, one Roman's hunger for the satisfactions of love.

The question at issue is not so much the value of Rome set against the value of Egypt, clear as these are, as it is the private relation between Antony and Cleopatra, a relation always colored by their different backgrounds and local loyalties. Normally speaking, it is not considered admirable, nor even sensible, for a man of public position to jeopardize his career for a woman. When the man is Antony, well-married in Rome and well-supplied elsewhere, and the woman Cleopatra, full of experience and of years, it is easy enough to see the matter with Roman eyes as a dissolute business between middle-aged sensualists having a last fling while they can, sinking into sloth and indolence and letting the affairs of empire go hang. Further, there is opportunism even in this love affair—that Cleopatra's political position was immensely strengthened by Antony's presence in Egypt, Caesar's sharp observations make plain. The suspicion certainly exists that she loves Antony for what he can do for her as well as for what he is to her.

The play begins with a Roman inductor, who takes the worst for granted. Philo (what a name for him!) evaluates the major characters according to accepted Roman standards; his critical speech breaks off as Antony and Cleopatra enter to act out what he has just, so degradingly, described as their typical behavior:

> Nay, but this dotage of our general's
> O'erflows the measure: those his goodly eyes,
> That o'er the files and musters of the war
> Have glow'd like plated Mars, now bend, now turn
> The office and devotion of their view
> Upon a tawny front: his captain's heart,
> Which in the scuffles of great fights hath burst
> The buckles on his breast, reneges all temper
> And is become the bellows and the fan
> To cool a gipsy's lust.
>   Look, where they come:
> Take but good note, and you shall see in him
> The triple pillar of the world transform'd
> Into a strumpet's fool: behold and see.
>
>   (1.1.1–13)

The hero and heroine then enter, to act out their tableau of mutual absorption. They behave with freedom towards each other—perhaps with abandon, indeed—but *not* as strumpet and fool. Their language, that of lovers bent on ideal expression, is thus quite counter to Philo's assessment of them:

> CLEOPATRA. If it be love indeed, tell me how much.
> ANTONY. There's beggary in love that can be reckon'd.
> CLEOPATRA. I'll set a bourn how far to be belov'd.
> ANTONY. Then must thou needs find out new heaven, new
>   earth.
>
>   (1.1.14–17)

The inflation of their language may strike us, but hardly as exceptional in any pair of lovers mutually absorbed. Rather, theirs is the common rhetoric of love, unspecified and generalized, seeking to express inexpressible heights and depths of feeling. Cosmic analogies are habitually called up by lovers less involved than these in the "real" world; the fact that Antony and Cleopatra are so deeply involved in the factual political world lends poignancy, irony, and a kind of accuracy to their occupational hyperbole. The "new heaven, new earth" of their love, created by them for themselves alone, must substitute for the real geography around them, the Mediterranean world over which their influence and the play's action range. Symbolic geography is invoked, with its real referents: Rome, Alexandria, Athens, Sicily, Sardinia, Parthia, Judea, Media, Mesopotamia, Syria, Armenia, Cyprus, Lydia, Cilicia, Phoenicia, Libya, Cappadocia, Paphlagonia, Thrace, Arabia, Pontus all testify to the reach of Rome, whose "universal peace," proclaimed by Caesar, was endangered by Antony's withdrawal from the world scene in wilful, careless, selfish pursuit of private satisfactions.

All this real world, then, was insufficient for these two—but more important than that, it was also too much for them. To keep their love safe, they must shut out the actual world in hopes of finding a new space for themselves small enough to exclude occupations other than love, large enough to contain their exalted imaginations. In this play, the common literary metaphor of lovers' giving up the world for love is taken as the literal donnée: meaning pours back to give substance to the cliché, as the play teaches something of the human cost involved in neglecting the serious public world, the glories and woes of war and administration, for love of one woman.

Antony and Cleopatra speak "excessively" from the beginning, in an idiom familiar enough in love-poetry. But it is worth noting that they are not alone in this habit of overstatement: Philo's initial speech is wholly cast in terms of excess. He degrades the amorous exploits of his commander with Egypt's queen, certainly: his account of that commander's military accomplishments is as excessive as his contumelious commentary on Antony's amatory achievements. Antony's eyes in war "glow'd like plated Mars"; "his captain's heart . . . burst the buckles on his breast." Caesar's speech too follows the pattern of overstatement: he makes the same kind of contrast of Antony's "lascivious wassails" and "tumblings on the bed of Ptolemy" to his astonishing endurance at Modena and on the Alps (1.4.55–71). Whatever Antony does, it seems, "o'erflows the measure"—but the Romans can *recognize* excess only in Antony's un-Roman acts: the heroic rest is, to them, natural in a Roman. Excess, then, is culturally conditioned: men recognize as excessive only what they regard as "too much," so that

Romans who valued military extravagance as much as Cleopatra valued extravagant pleasures could find in her Antony much to praise. When Octavius denounces Antony's self-indulgence, he calls him "A man who is the abstract of all faults / That all men follow." Who could be more than this, an epitome of ill? Taking exception to Octavius's statement, Lepidus casts his comments in terms equally hyperbolical:

> I must not think there are
> Evils enow to darken all his goodness:
> His faults in him, seem as the spots of heaven,
> More fiery by night's blackness.
>
> (1.4.10–13)

What are we to make of Antony, then? What are we to make of his present love-experience, judged by Philo as tawdry and low, judged by the lovers as quite past the reach of expression? In fact, what do Antony and Cleopatra *do*? We are told (by Romans) how they pass their time, in behavior characterized as "Asiatic" in the extreme. Egypt is, certainly, "the East," regularly so designated in the play. As queen, Cleopatra is often addressed by her country's name; when she dies, she is called "the eastern star," that is, the planet Venus. What Antony and Cleopatra do, evidently, is live by the attributes of the Asiatic style; they act out, they and the Romans tell us, a life-style gaudy, loose, ungirt, decorated, artful, contrived, and deceitful. The Egyptian court is an idle, opulent, sensual, Asiatic place, where men are effeminate and women bold. Mardian the eunuch exists to remind us of what can happen to a man in such an environment, and we see Antony unmanned in various symbolic ways. Normal decorum is constantly breached by this general, this queen. Drunk, Antony will not hear his messages from Rome; playing with Cleopatra, he relinquishes his armor to her and dresses in her "tires and mantles." She takes his sword away, and though she returns it before their battle, she disarms him entirely in the midst of a real battle, by more critical means. Publicly she ignores him, however preoccupied with him privately. Nor is she manly, for all the dressing in armor and proclaiming herself a man's equal before the last battle. At Actium she flees out of fear, and retires in the last pitch as well: when Antony is dying before her eyes, she will not emerge from her monument, nor even open its doors that he may easily be brought in to her—because, she says, she is afraid.

In Egypt men feast and sleep. "The beds in the East are soft" in many ways. Both defeat and victory are celebrated in Egypt by one other gaudy night, and Caesar seems to acknowledge this Egyptian need for self-indulgence when, to reassure the captive Cleopatra, he urges her to "Feed and sleep." Though the meanings of "sleep" deepen radically by the end of the play, at the beginning and for the most part, "sleep" is a sign of Egyptian indolence and womanishness. Festivities are unmanly too; Caesar says of his great competitor:

> From Alexandria
> This is the news: he fishes, drinks, and wastes
> The lamps of night in revel; is not more manlike
> Than Cleopatra; nor the queen of Ptolemy
> More womanly than he.
>
> (1.4.3–7)

His last comment may indicate Caesar's limitations as a judge of human character, but it also sums up the Roman attitude to Egypt, a place merely of "lascivious wassails." The way most Romans think of Cleopatra, it is no wonder that she shrinks, at the end, from being carried through Rome to see "some squeaking Cleopatra boy my greatness / I' the posture of a whore." She knows how she is named in Rome, because in his rage Antony tells her:

> I found you as a morsel, cold upon
> Dead Caesar's trencher; nay, you were a fragment
> Of Gnaeus Pompey's, besides what hotter hours,
> Unregister'd in vulgar fame, you have
> Luxuriously pick'd out.
>
> (3.13.116–20)

Again and again, "appetite" is a word used to cover all satisfactions. Feasting and love (or, better, sex) are equated, as in the passage just quoted. Cleopatra is often reduced to food—by Enobarbus, speaking of Antony, "He will to his Egyptian dish again"; by herself, in her youth "a morsel for a monarch," although those were, as she says, her "salad days," when she was both greener and colder than she later became. Pompey speaks man-to-man to Antony of "your fine Egyptian cookery" (2.7.63–65) and, later, of the "cloyless sauce" that Egypt proves for Antony.

Unquestionably the preoccupation with sex and with the shared sexuality of Antony and Cleopatra runs as an undercurrent through the play. The difference between Egyptian and Roman talk of sex is instructive: Charmian and the Soothsayer, Cleopatra and the Eunuch, speak playfully and naturally; Enobarbus speaks cynically to and about Antony, on "death," on horses and mares; and the other Romans show their prurience and crudity when they speak, as they compulsively do, about the subject. The imagery too carries its sexual meanings: Cleopatra's "sweating labour" joins with the imagery of bearing and of weight to remind us of the woman's part in the act of love. This language in turn conjoins with the marvelous and varied horse-imagery which reaches its peak as she imagines the absent Antony on horseback: "O happy horse, to bear the weight of Antony!" Such language assumes sexuality to be a normal part of life; the Nile-imagery, with its "quickenings" and "foison" references, suggests procreation and creation as part of a natural cycle. Nature provides reproductive images for sexuality, and war another sort. The constant reference to swords, in fact as in image, keeps manliness ever at the forefront of our awareness, as it is at the forefront of the dramatic characters' awareness, too.

There is more than the suggestion, then, that love is no more than appetite or a drive; if that were all there was to love, the Roman view of this affair would be correct, Cleopatra simply a whore and Antony besotted, "ne'er lust-wearied." But can a man remain "ne'er lust-wearied" by the same woman, however infinite her variety, if she is merely a whore, however aristocratic her birth? Enobarbus, in so many ways faithful to Antony and Cleopatra in spite of his disapproval of their behavior, sees something more in her and tries to say what that "more" is. Once again, significantly, he speaks in terms of food— "Other women cloy / The appetites they feed, but she makes hungry,/ Where most she satisfies." Mere sexuality, strong sexual love, idealized love: however it is described, the emotions shared by Antony and Cleopatra challenge the heroic world of Roman military organization.

This miracle of love (or whatever it is) we do not see acted out onstage. Indeed, we never see Antony and Cleopatra alone, as we do Romeo and Juliet, Desdemona and Othello. What we see is something quite different: a man and a woman playing, quarreling, making up; a woman sulking, pretending to anger, flying into real rages, running away from danger, flirting even in deep disgrace and danger. Except on Roman tongues, there is little that can be called shameless or lascivious in Cleopatra's or Antony's utterances about love: her language on this preoccupying subject is remarkably clean—which is not the case with Roman commentators on these spectacular lovers.

To make so commonplace, so vulgar a mixture into a woman worth losing the world for is a considerable task for any playwright. Our playwright accomplishes it by fairly simple, even domestic, means. His Cleopatra has, among other things, a girlish, hoydenish companionability. She is obviously amusing company; she will try anything once. She has a lovely imagination and considerable command of language. She tries to rise to occasions, and sometimes she does. We hear much of Cleopatra's whoredom, and we see Antony blundering after her, twice fatally; we hear him speak of the less pleasant side of his love, of the "Egyptian fetters" which tie him in Alexandria, of his "dotage," and later, when he misses her in Rome, of his "pleasure" with Cleopatra. There is every reason to think very little of Cleopatra—although, to balance her crudities (as when she had a salt-fish attached to Antony's line), we are made to see that even in her breaches of decorum, her riggishness, her foolish middle age, she is delightful. She is earthy, and down-to-earth; her sudden accessions of realism puncture both the romanticizing of the lovers and Antony's simplistic view of love and Cleopatra as satisfaction to his appetite. This woman is something more:

> Sir, you and I must part . . .
> Sir, you and I have lov'd.
> (1.3.87–88)

> In praising Antony, I have disprais'd Caesar . . .
> I am paid for't now.
>
> (2.5.107–9)

> Think you there was, or might be such a man
> As this I dreamt of?
>
> (5.2.93–94)

> Antony
> Shall be brought drunken forth, and I shall see
> Some squeaking Cleopatra boy my greatness
> I' the posture of a whore.
> (5.2.218–20)

When her ironical common sense pierces her own theatricals, her charm is irresistible: though she rarely acts on that knowledge, we see that at moments she knows herself and the precarious, politicking world she lives in. It is this side of her, the practical, real woman, that

is picked up in Charmian's farewell epithet: to "a *lass* unparallel'd."
Age, apparently, could not wither her, nor a rakish life, nor childbearing.

But in her first parting from Antony, as in her exchange with
Dolabella after Antony's death and just before her own, Cleopatra's
common sense rises to something greater:

> Sir, you and I must part, but that's not it:
> Sir, you and I have lov'd, but there's not it.

The facts are clear enough—but they do not provide Cleopatra with an
explanation for the pressure of her feelings, that this love for Antony is
unduly significant, that parting from him must radically diminish her.
Her sentence loses its direction as she seeks to express the "more" of
her feeling for him:

> That you know well, something it is I would,—
> O, my oblivion is a very Antony,
> And I am all forgotten!
>
> (1.3.89–91)

As she later says, she wants to sleep out "the great gap of time" that
Antony is away from her; in his absence, even by herself, she is, imagina-
tively, "forgotten" and therefore does not exist. Both Antony and Cleopatra
speak feelingly and movingly about their sense of identity lost. Part of
their tragedy lies in Antony's feeling himself dissolve when he is with
her, and Cleopatra's feeling her "nothingness" when he is not with her.

Cleopatra makes clear that her love for Antony is fully sexual;
but, as has been noted, this emphasis comes in reverie, not in lascivious action or exchange. What is significant, surely, is that in a life
given to sexual conquest and enjoyment, her relation to Antony means
more to her than anything else. It is not that Cleopatra does not want
to be reminded of her old connection with Caesar; it is that she knows
its qualitative difference from the connection with Antony. Certainly
Cleopatra does not shirk the facts of her sexual past; however giddy
and irresponsible her behavior with Antony, though, she knows that
for him, she has quit being a rake. For her, sexuality is never just the
"pleasure" that Antony implies early in the play it is for him. It has (at
last, one has the impression) risen above itself to become love of a sort
that defies definition in psychological ways, not just in "literary"
ways. Indeed, in literary ways, the lovers' extreme preoccupation with
one another is almost *too* resonant to the conventional language of
love: as in *Othello,* but in an entirely different context, the Petrarchan

mixture of love and war has here been actualized in the necessary conditions, unmetaphored into actuality, of everyday life for this general and this queen. But the love-poet's transcendent aim is the same as theirs: how to express the indefinable love they share, a love that to unsympathetic onlookers seems ordinary enough, vulgar enough, but to the lover experiencing it inexpressibly glorious and valuable. Their language is pitched at the familiar literary goal, to make the "new heaven, new earth" of lovers' cliché into a universe for their exclusive dwelling. Their *folie à deux* is in part a matter of language, manipulated to record heightened experience and to displace both conventional and particular renditions of their experience by others.

Cleopatra's imagination particularly works at this task: if sex is the reality and imagination the fantasy of love, then the two fuse in Cleopatra's speech in Antony's absence from her, when she imagines him as he at that very moment actually *is*:

> Stands he, or sits he?
> Or does he walk? or is he on his horse?
>
> (1.5.19–20)

Her sexual memories crowd into the single line, "O happy horse, to bear the weight of Antony!" Her images of weight, realistic enough in any woman's experience of love, come to their culmination in the terrible scene of Antony's death, as she draws him into her monument:

> How heavy weighs my lord!
> Our strength is all gone into heaviness,
> That makes the weight.
>
> (4.15.32–34)

The reality is there, although not displayed to us, of the children she has borne him; "the lap of Egypt's widow," as Pompey so rudely said, has actually held Antony and known what it was to do so. Finally, to her "demi-Atlas" she attributes more weight than any man can carry; she turns her love into an even more colossal personage than the world will recognize or can, in the person of Dolabella, accept.

In this habit of stretching expression, of trying to say more than words or figures habitually allow, lies some clue to the effect on each other of these lovers. They make each other feel that age is no bar to living fully; they make each other feel, not still alive, but more than usually alive, a feeling, however illusory, which can exercise curious power over a man and a woman more than commonly experienced. The connection between them, obviously, is quite different from other experiences they have had; Cleopatra knows this from the beginning of the play, and we witness Antony coming to know it too. It is precisely his marriage to Octavia, with all its chilly merits, that teaches him what Cleopatra is to him. In their view of each other, Antony and Cleopatra are more than life-size. So Cleopatra speaks truth in her great speech of hyperbole about Antony:

> I dreamt there was an Emperor Antony.
> O such another sleep, that I might see
> But such another man! . . .
> His face was as the heavens, and therein stuck
> A sun and moon, which kept their course, and lighted
> The little O, the earth. . . .
> His legs bestrid the ocean, his rear'd arm
> Crested the world: his voice was propertied
> As all the tuned spheres, and that to friends:
> But when he meant to quail, and shake the orb,
> He was as rattling thunder. For his bounty,
> There was no winter in 't: an autumn 'twas
> That grew the more by reaping: his delights
> Were dolphin-like, they show'd his back above
> The element they liv'd in: in his livery
> Walk'd crowns and crownets: realms and islands were
> As plates dropp'd from his pocket.
>
> (5.2.76–92)

Antony has then finally turned into that "new heaven, new earth" he had told Cleopatra in the first scene she must find as the appropriate bound of their love. Microcosm and macrocosm change places: the earth is smaller than this man, as the common cosmic metaphor expands into all space and more-than-time in the images of ever-ripe autumn and a creature, the dolphin, transcending his natural element. Correspondence imagery involving worlds in different scales—the cosmos, however thought of; macrocosm and microcosm; stars and eyes—is so common in sixteenth- and seventeenth-century poetry as to be mere cliché, and certainly at one level, all Cleopatra is doing in this magnificent speech is making more extravagant a notion already hyperbolical at its base. But in this particular case of lovers, the standard hyperbole has its peculiar reality to "match" this particular psychological and political situation. In the imagery, the larger world has been contracted into the limits of Antony's body (normally a microcosm), and Antony's body in turn enlarged encompasses and surpasses the macrocosm to which originally it had been likened. In fact, this is what happened to these lovers: "the world," in this case half or a third of the civilized world which was under their control, was rejected in favor of the "little world," quite literally, of man. "Bodies" are very important in the play, and although Antony and Cleopatra speak with remarkable delicacy about each other's bodies and their own bodily sensations in love, this speech gives the literary justification for that physical love. Hyperbolic metaphor that it is, this speech at the same time unmetaphors its literary content by making plain the crucial importance to these lovers of their finite, particular, well-worn bodies.

Cleopatra does not linger on the fantasy, but asks Dolabella, with the realism characteristic of her:

> Think you there was, or might be such a man
> As this I dreamt of?
>
> (5.2.93–94)

To that, Roman Dolabella can only respond, "Gentle madam, no"—which serves to arouse Cleopatra to still more immense reaches of imagery, to language rejecting anything nature can offer as fit comparison to the wonder that Antony was. This time momentary realism touched off, as it habitually does not, the reassertion of hyperbole's value. Hyperbole becomes "true"—and yet even that hyperbolical language is not "enough" for the intense feelings between these two overreachers of life. In the references within the play, they are always more than merely human, more than triumvir and queen: Cleopatra was, we hear, more beautiful than the most beautiful picture of Venus. Art cannot render her, nor can nature's works render Antony. In her eulogy of him, Cleopatra never denies his manhood—"My man of men," she says, and she should know—but the manhood she attributes to him no ordinary mortal can aspire to. His bounty was endless—and his treatment of Enobarbus suggests that this is so—his delights transcendent. His empire was to be prodigal of imperial power—"as plates dropp'd from his pocket." Compare that magnificence with Caesar's careful accounting of Mark Antony's distribution of empire in act 3, scene 6: for Caesar, these political entities which Mark Antony gave away were no mere "plates" but the extended possessions of Rome, to be protected, at cost, for Rome's sake.

Cleopatra's imagination is as bountiful as Antony's generosity. Her language is rich as her habitat, and she is, as both detractors and admirers point out, histrionic to a degree. She stages herself at Cydnus; she stages herself as dead for Antony; she stages herself for her death. She speaks and is spoken of in theatrical terms of scene, act, and stage; she is a creature of impulse and whim, which she tries out on her audiences, acting to Dolabella, to Caesar, to Antony, acting even with her familiar maids. That habit of acting stands her in good stead in her determination to outwit Caesar at the end. Reversing Marx's famous quip, this play first acts out in farce what becomes tragedy a second time through. Cleopatra pretends to be dead—trivially, but with horrible results for Antony—before she dies in earnest. The theme of death echoes throughout the play—the lovers know, long before the crisis, the cost of their choice. Enobarbus plays on the slang term, "death," for sexual intercourse, when Antony first tells him he must be gone; his cynicism can seem justified to an audience which sees Cleopatra feign illness and death. Her coquetry, charming within the domestic protections of her court, is fatal on the battlefield. It is worth noting that for the deceit which cost him his life, Mark Antony never reproaches her; instead, he promises to be "A bridegroom in my death, and run into 't / As to a lover's bed." She too equates love and death: "The stroke of death is as a lover's pinch, / Which hurts, and is desir'd." She dies to join Mark Antony—"Husband, I come"—as his wife, taking for granted the meaning of a simple act which could never take place in the Roman world during their lives. Put in the simplest terms, the word "death" is gradually ennobled by what happens in the play—but not before its seamier implications have all been laid before us.

So the play begins to live up to itself. As Philo's crudity is submerged under the lovers' flood of words, again and again the nasty turns out to have its noble aspect too, the Gorgon indeed becomes Mars. Because the playwright never shirks the unpleasantness, the triviality, even the occasional brutality of the lovers, because he always allows them to recognize and to reveal the compulsiveness of their love, its literal extremity, that love's peculiar force begins to take its confirmation from the radical action and the extreme language. As we watch the hyperbole coming true, we recognize a maturing of emotions more than life-size to begin with, commanding a space of their own making, relying on their mutual respect for their own worth. The simplicity, singleheartedness, and intensity of this faulty human love, magnificent in spite of the lovers' politics and duplicity, in spite of the inevitable deceits of their world, come to seem a far greater achievement, against greater odds, than the successful Roman quest for power.

And for this, as we shall see, there is theoretical precedent in Longinus's defense of the style Antony and his acquaintances used, a style designed to express generosity, magnitude, magnanimity; a style, as he put it, "with the true ring of a noble mind." Though Shakespeare does not slight the cultural structure and construction of any style— Roman, Egyptian here, Navarrese elsewhere—he is concerned in this play with the significance of a personal style within the cultural matrix, with what Longinus called "μεγαλοφροσύνη." Though we know, from Philo's initial speech, of Antony's capacity for greatness and perceive, in his dealings with Enobarbus and Cleopatra, his magnanimity in the face of terrible losses, he still has to live up to the nobility of his soul and to the elevation of his speech. Still more Cleopatra, unused to Roman gestures of magnanimity: from riggish, rakish queen who plays tricks with a man's honor and his life, she must grow into the moral capacities her hyperbole seems to make light of.

The risks are great—how does a man, how can a woman, leave off grandiose and bombastic play-acting, even to the roles of god and goddess, to die as heroes? The lovers set their sights high from the start: chose as their models superhuman figures from Roman mythology—Antony in the play's first speech is likened to Mars, Cleopatra unmistakably to Venus. They act out that archetypal coupling throughout their lives, even to receiving mockery like the gods of Venus and Mars. Cleopatra is a goddess of love in her disguises, both the Roman Venus and the Egyptian Isis: she celebrated her greatest political triumph, over Antony and by his means over Rome, dressed "in the habiliments of the goddess Isis," as Caesar in outrage reports. Isis was also a moon-goddess, whose variability, reflected in the feminine psychology, is made much of in the play; her "habiliments," as Plutarch tells us in another place, are varicolored, to show her involvement with all nature—with light as well as dark, fire as well as water, life as well as death, beginning as well as ending. These robes are singularly appropriate to Cleopatra: they symbolize all matter and "afford many disclosures of themselves, and opportunities to view them as they are changed about in various ways." Cleopatra is too much a woman, variable and faulty, to "be" either Venus or Isis, but she takes the part of both of them; posing as these goddesses, she occasionally takes on some of their meanings, as Antony on occasion takes on some of the meanings attributed to Mars and Hercules. In addition, this pair is too intermingled in one another for such an interpretation: whatever their natural attributes making them godlike, Antony and Cleopatra are a man and a woman to each other and to the world.

Although it is as a man that she most values him, Cleopatra symbolically and actually unmans Antony. We hear of her dressing him in her clothes, as Omphale did Hercules. His decline from perfect manhood to something less than that is part of Antony's tragedy. In this play, however, the facts of the Roman idea of manhood are examined again and again and found wanting, particularly in respect to the very quality Antony so lavishly displays, magnanimity. He was a generous, a prodigal man, but always a man large of spirit. Largesse is his attribute, in all senses. He gave away his goods to his soldiers in defeat; his graciousness drove the defected Enobarbus to his shamefast death. To Antony's naturally great character Octavius stands in cheerless contrast; and no one in Rome, ever, is shown as rising to Antony's heights of grace. Again and again we are brought up against the hard realization that if to be a Roman is to be so narrow and calculating as Octavius, so vulgar as Pompey, so divided as Enobarbus, then Antony has surely chosen the better part. Octavius speaks beautifully of Antony's death:

> The breaking of so great a thing should make
> A greater crack. The round world
> Should have shook lions into civil streets,
> And citizens to their dens. The death of Antony
> Is not a single doom; in the name lay
> A moiety of the world.
>
> (5.1.14–19)

Beautiful words indeed to eulogize a dead colleague and opponent— but Caesar cannot help calculating the man's worth: "A moiety of the world." That coveted demi-monde is at last his; the reckoning is over, the world brought under Caesar's universal landlordism. The "boy" has become, as Cleopatra names him, "Sole sir of the world." After the briefest respite in honor of his dead "mate in empire," Caesar turns back to the business of the world and lays his plans for the future. To such a man, it is difficult not to prefer the prodigal old ruffian, who can assert, and mean it, "There's beggary in love that can be reckon'd," who can risk and lose his moiety (or his third) of the world for something which, however flawed, he valued above himself.

For Antony is no standard Roman, as the Romans testify. Men *speak* of his greatness of character and action, his stature in virtue and in vice. Men *act* to honor those qualities: his soldiers love him; his servant kills himself rather than stab his master; Enobarbus dies of having betrayed him. Philo can speak of him only in hyperbolical terms; so, in spite of themselves, can Caesar and Lepidus. In everyone's mind, this man was aggrandized and enlarged above the commonalty of men. Like his ancestor Hercules, Antony does things no other man can do, on a scale on which no other man can do them. It is not Cleopatra alone who feels this, but everyone who knows him. When we compare this Antony with the man duped twice by Cleopatra, or with the man causing Caesar's messenger to be beaten, or the man feasting, joking, and making love with Cleopatra, we see the range of the problem Shakespeare set himself—and we must suspect that some of this hyperbole is merely bombast. But when his imagination is fired by Cleopatra, Antony *can* do great deeds at arms. He conquered the entire East and redistributed its countries (without consulting Rome) among Cleopatra and her children. When she arms him, he defeats the Romans at odds, and returns to tell her his "gests" that day. At his death, when an ordinary man might well have nagged, he looks to an Elysium in which he and she shall outdo Aeneas and Dido; he warns her to look after her safety and, like the great lover he is, dies on a kiss. No trace remains of his rage at her, no trace of reproach for her false message: with his own life he was prodigal; with hers, he was generous.

These are the gestures to match an hyperbolical style, the behavior so admired by Longinus: the gestures of the overreaching man whose imagination is larger than the stage it must act upon. For Antony, the two "stand up peerless"; Cleopatra remembers that

> Eternity was in our lips, and eyes,
> Bliss in our brow's bent; none our parts so poor,
> But was a race of heaven.
>
> (1.3.35–37)

For her he was, finally, truly Herculean, a "demi-Atlas," a colossus whose "legs bestrid the ocean"; he was greater than the arch of empire itself: he was her world. For him, she could make herself into Venus and Isis, could "be" ageless and infinitely desirable, immortal, more than human. They read their stature from their mutual view of one another. Their ideas of themselves and of each other may have been unrealistic, vain, self-flattering, and self-deceitful, but they reflected what can never be readily explained, the peculiar sense of well-being and power a man and woman in love can give each other. So their clumsy games, their open lovemaking and open quarreling, their flirtations, their drinking, their mockery, turn somehow from nonsense and bombast into legitimate hyperbole, into a language forever on the stretch to express what had not been expressed before. Far from ideal lovers, Antony and Cleopatra demand a language for their love which rejects conventional hyperbole and invents and creates new overstatements, new forms of overstatement. In the language itself, we can read the insatiability of their love, as the language seems to make hungry, too, where most it satisfies. Nothing is enough for these two, not even the most extravagant figures of speech.

The language Antony and Cleopatra use, the language others use about them, is stretched at its upper and lower limits, to express their high and low gestures as bigger than lifesize. It is interesting that Antony and Cleopatra do not bewitch others' imaginations only by their charismatic presence; their great qualities are praised, described, referred to, and criticized mostly in their absence. These two are watched by a world fascinated even when disapproving; they are staged in a play of their own making, with the world as their willing audience. But they do not really play for that audience: their imaginative acting is all for each other, and in their mutual absorption they do not care who happens to look on at the spectacle. Of course the Romans cannot keep their eyes off them; beneath the language of official disapproval, one can see Roman fascination with this un-Roman style of life, with this abundant, prodigal, excessive manner of doing things. Their bounty knows no winter but is, in Antony's word, always "foison."

Ripeness, overripeness: certainly the images of fertility, in particular the Nile-imagery, stresses life-giving, fecundity, creation; and, with these good qualities, also corruption and rotting. Action can corrupt; so can inaction. In Caesar's image for the variable Roman people, the famous "vagabond flag" passage, we read of one kind of rotting; in Antony's inaction we see another. The flag is dissolved in the stream's current; "solutus," dissolved, was one word of disapprobation applied to the Asiatic style, and (as Charney points out) images of dissolution and deliquescence abound in the play. We see things dissolve and resolve—the liaison with Cleopatra, the marriage with Octavia. Antony vacillates between his Roman alliances and his Egyptian delights, choosing now the one, now the other. The tide is against him, literally at Actium, figuratively on land as well. And yet one is not surprised at this particular literalization of water-images of dissolution, for the metaphor has gained power through the play until, in Antony's great speech about himself, we see that he thinks of himself as formless, his shape lost. The metaphor of dissolution is overtly made use of through the play—"Let Rome in Tiber melt," Antony cries at the beginning; "Authority melts from me," he says near the end of his life. Cleopatra too speaks in this image: "Melt Egypt into Nile." If she should ever play him false, then "dissolve my life." Both use the neologism "discandy," Cleopatra in a hyperbolical assertion of love, Antony in connection with his melting authority:

> The hearts
> That spaniel'd me at heels, to whom I gave
> Their wishes, do discandy, melt their sweets
> On blossoming Caesar.
>
> (4.12.20–23)

The most important of the dissolution passages is Antony's speech about himself as a cloud in which shapes continually shift, dissolve, and reform until "The rack dislimns, and makes it indistinct, / As water is in water." When he finds his Roman form again and dies "a Roman, by a Roman / Valiantly vanquish'd," Cleopatra says of him, "The crown o' the earth doth melt," into a nothingness she feels as palpable. To mark Cleopatra's death, Charmian calls for cosmic dissolution, "Dissolve, thick cloud, and rain, that I may say / The gods themselves do weep" (5.2.298–99).

Peculiarly enough, other words characteristically applied in denigration to the Asiatic style are picked up and openly developed in the powerful imagery of this play. "Enervis" is such a word—Antony and Cleopatra taunt each other with idleness (1.2.113–14, 127; 3.8.90–92), and Antony accuses himself of "slackness" (3.7.27). The notion of effeminacy is related to the notion of idleness and, in Enobarbus's last speech to Antony, is explicitly connected with melting. Enobarbus weeps ("I, an ass, am onion-eyed"), and asks Antony to stop talking—"for shame / Transform us not to women" (4.2.35–36). "Inanis," empty, is another word played in the imagery: "vacancy" occurs, in connection with voluptuousness (1.4.26), and in Enobarbus's attempt to praise Cleopatra (2.6.216). By all odds the most significant use in the play of such a term is the imagery and the practice of enlargement, of blowing up. The Asiatic style was "inflatus": we have seen how Cleopatra continually enlarged her idea of Antony, until in her paean to Dolabella of Antony's greatness she outdid her hyperbolical habits of rhetoric. There is, too, much about inflation in the play's language. In the first speech of Philo, in which so much of the play's implications, sexual and other, lie coiled, Antony is said to have "become the bellows and the fan / To cool a gipsy's lust." Primarily, the bellows blows up, the fan cools: but *both* can actually blow up and both can cool. On her barge, Cleopatra has magical fans, apparently, also both blowing and cooling: the "winds did seem / To glow the delicate cheeks which they did cool, / And what they undid did." (2.2.203–5). Breathless, Cleopatra breathes forth her power; in her, Enobarbus assures his hearers, defect becomes perfection. Antony and Cleopatra, then, "inflate" each other—or, to put the same thing more gracefully, they inspirit each other. For those Atticists who polemicized against the Asiatic style, such "inflation" was bad because it was untrue to nature and gave false impressions of fact. Now, Antony and Cleopatra may have had, and have fostered, false impressions about themselves and each other; but they were trying to do something else, something highly respectable and highly poetic: to give utterance to their own convictions and sensations of being larger than life, which in turn demanded a style of expression more spacious than that used by the ruck of mankind. By means of the style, ever on the reach for an undefined "more," the infinite longings of these figures can be understood: but, furthermore, by means of this twice-heightened speech, the play examines not only the values of an enriched style, but the values of the life it seeks to match. The play is a study in richness and ripeness, necessarily also a study in overripeness as well, a study even of corruption. But never may we conclude, in morality vein, that these last qualities are valueless, that the people who speak so are simply megalomaniac and self-deluded. Indeed, what emerges from the play is something quite different, the affirmation of the values, qualified by an awareness of its dangers, of such a way of life.

As one works through the play, several things become clearer: at the beginning, Antony speaks hyperbolically, bombastically: his honest heartfelt emotions, mingled with an ironic self-criticism, are reserved for his realization of Fulvia's death. It is Cleopatra who checks his overstatement, questions the sincerity of his hyperbole ("Excellent falsehood"; "Hear the ambassadors"). Mocking him, she is still besotted with him; no less than Antony is she manipulable by her love. Both Antony and Cleopatra suffer from self-surpassing rages, she at the messenger, he at her apparent and real betrayals of him; hyperbole operates there in both language and gesture. By the third act, something has begun to happen which demonstrates the identity of the lovers: the hyperbolical style with which Antony began the play now issues from Cleopatra's mouth:

> Ah, dear, if I be so,
> From my cold heart let heaven engender hail,
> And poison it in the source, and the first stone
> Drop in my neck: as it determines, so
> Dissolve my life; the next Caesarion smite
> Till by degrees the memory of my womb,
> Together with my brave Egyptians all,
> By the discandying of this pelleted storm,
> Lie graveless, till the flies and gnats of Nile
> Have buried them for prey!
>
> (3.13.158–67)

It is Antony now who says, "I am satisfied," evidently needing that assurance to go on with the "chronicle" of which he feels himself to be a part. Early in the play, Antony and Cleopatra are separately hyperbolical; as their unity grows, they adapt to each other's modes of speech. These lovers are in many ways temperamentally alike, and they become more so as their meaning for each other becomes more conscious and more motivating in their lives. In the third act, as they pitch their lives together once more, their most hyperbolical speeches of love are signs of their deepening unity with one another, the more poignant for their violent and frequent misunderstandings.

To speak as they do, so grandly, so magnificently, so frankly in hyperbole, is in Antony's and Cleopatra's nature. They are true to one aspect of the Attic (or "Senecan") prescription, after all, in that they express "themselves" truly in their language—this is to say, then, that their style *must* in honesty be bombastic, which according to Attic prescription should mean that their style matches the variability and shoddiness of their characters, discovers beneath their bluster and shouting mere fustian cheapness, secondhand emotions, and sleasy intentions. Longinus was fully aware of how close the elevated style was to bombast: it is almost as if Shakespeare set himself to examine

Longinus's problem fully in this play, to test out against human actions and human speech the human aspiration for sublimity.

Antony's habits of speech reach toward and respond to the fundamental grandeur of his nature, as his actions increasingly confirm the propriety and integrity of his grand style. That Enobarbus adopts the hyperbolical mode—that Plutarch adopts it, indeed—to render Cleopatra's magnificence, tells us much about the "real" application of an inflated and hyperbolical style. In Enobarbus's mouth we are invited to recognize things as they are: Enobarbus knows *ping* from *pong*, Rome from Egypt. For better and for worse, Enobarbus is a Roman, speaks as a Roman, acts as a Roman. Yet to this man is given the great speech about Cleopatra, its figures stretching farther and farther as the speech goes on and as he realizes the difficulties involved in making anyone who has not experienced her charm understand what this woman is. Like his master, vacillating between Rome and Egypt in his own life, Enobarbus seems to opt for Rome against Egypt. At his end he chooses neither place, but rather chooses a man, a human being involved with both symbolic places and, for him, transcending both. From his relation to Mark Antony, Enobarbus took his final definition, to die with his betrayed master's name on his lips. By the pull of hyperbole, of overstatement, of inflation, and of magnanimity on such a man, we can measure the power of Antony for Cleopatra—and, just because of his greatness, can measure her power for him. The two lovers confirm each other and themselves—so much we might expect. Enobarbus, with his excursions beyond his habitual style and behavior, not wanting to do so, nonetheless confirms them from outside themselves.

In his set-speech on Cleopatra, Enobarbus had called upon a natural miracle to attest to her power:

> Antony
> Enthron'd i' the market-place, did sit alone,
> Whistling to the air; which, but for vacancy,
> Had gone to gaze on Cleopatra too,
> And made a gap in nature.
>
> (2.2.214–18)

Even in figure, though, this miracle cannot take place: there is no gap in nature, nor in this play, however crowded things are by the space Antony and Cleopatra take up, by the bruit of their presence, the bustle of their companionship. To stretch the metaphor, the play's dominant style is not one of vanity, although there are vanities enough blatantly set forth in the protagonists' characters. They are self-centered and self-indulgent—but they are not self-satisfied. They look to each other forever for more; they criticize each other and themselves. In their lives, however lived out in the Asiatic style, in dissoluteness, inflation, swelling, enervation, slackness, effeminacy, and idleness, these two do *not* decay. Their satisfactions breed hunger; their desire neither stales nor cloys, not even at the moments in which they die. Finally, their desire can be seen to be a particular kind of love, a kind of love rarely made romantic, firmly based in shared sexual experience. Out of such love, each can think only of the other at the time of death.

Even when they are idle, Antony and Cleopatra make a stir in the world. This is perhaps part of the tragedy (though not in Renaissance terms): that public figures cannot afford private joys. In the modern jargon, there is no solution to their problems either of aspiring temperament or of historical situation. They could not do without each other and, their world being what it was, they could not live comfortably with each other. But imagine alternative solutions: suppose Antony *had* gone back to live in Rome with Octavia and their daughters (present in Plutarch but excised from the play); the political struggle with Caesar could hardly have failed to come to a head, for Caesar, if not Antony, had to find opportunity for quarrel. Suppose Cleopatra had gone back to her philanderings with Eastern potentates and Roman ambassadors: could she have restrained herself from political troublemaking, out of boredom if nothing else? Or, turning the matter about still more, how could Antony have lived among Romans whose view of Cleopatra was as extreme as his own, though at quite the other end of the scale? Could he have endured the silliness of Lepidus, the calculations of Octavius, the prurience of Menas and the rest, their eagerness to vulgarize personal experiences beyond their capacities to imagine? Character has something to do with "fate"—the struggle with Caesar would have come in the end, without the satisfaction for Antony of having chosen for Cleopatra, without the heroics at his death which, self-deceiving or not, eased him into Elysium with the conviction that his life had been worth its trouble and pain, and that his final disgrace was canceled by his grandiose final gestures of love.

This is a curious play, resting on an ambivalent concept of love impossible to sum up, to categorize, or to define. We learn throughout that desire can remain insatiable, that vacillation breeds corruption, that rewards in one sphere exact penalties in another. Cleopatra's fans heated where they cooled, what they undid, did. So Cleopatra: she undid Antony, but also she made of him not so much what she wanted him to be—indeed, in that she failed—as what *he* wanted to be. Certainly one cannot draw as a general conclusion from this play that an intense connection between a man and a woman justifies all else, justifies all the neglect, the idleness, the betrayals, the prodigality of lives and honor. Shakespeare shows us, unmistakably, that it does not, by the play's eternal balancing of one thing against another, its long vacillation between the bombastic and the sublime, its constant qualification of virtue by fault, of vice by virtue. But on balance, it is obvious that those experiences, from whatever source, which can elevate human beings are judged more favorably than those which do not; that those human beings who can be elevated are nobler than those whose nature is too small to permit such enlargement. With all its qualifications and all its defects admitted, proclaimed, displayed, the love of Antony and Cleopatra is nonetheless affirmed, the strumpet and the strumpet's fool grow into the imaginative warrior and the theatrical queen. There is no denying their excesses, which are examined, studied, and reassessed both by the speakers within the play and by the audience watching the excesses demonstrated onstage. We learn that in such excess, life itself can reside. Though it threatens to rot, and seems at times to have corrupted the lovers, their style of living affirms their life—and that despite the deaths of the proceedings.

Indeed, in the deaths we see the value of the lives. Antony says that he dies as a Roman, but he bungled his death all the same, both by letting Eros die before him, and by not killing himself outright. However significant the "elevation" of Antony into Cleopatra's tomb, it is an awkward business; the queen's failure to open the tomb lays stress, just at the worst moment, on the weakest side of her nature. Antony's dying skirts bombast the while, and we may assume that his failure to die efficiently in the Roman style is one mark Egypt laid upon him.

His beauty of character, though, emerges clearly through this uncomfortable death-scene: in spite of the clumsiness, what we remember is Antony's magnanimity and Cleopatra's high poetry. Antony affirms in his manner of dying both the Roman and the Eastern sides of his nature; Cleopatra too comes to accept Roman ways, even to embrace them in her own death. Her contemptuous fear of "Roman thoughts" in the first act gives way before her desire to emulate Antony and to die, like him, "in the high Roman fashion." Her suicide, though, cannot be said to be pure Roman: she had done research into painless ways to die; she chose the Nile worm as a suitable weapon; she arranged the spectacle of her death with a care and love inappropriate to Roman suicide. In both suicides, a Roman pattern has been expanded and enriched by Egyptian opulence and Egyptian decoration, not least in the ornate style in which both Antony and Cleopatra take leave of their world. The actual world has shrunk away from them; in expectation of Elysium in each other's company, they affirm the larger world of their fantastic and extravagant imagination, which their love had brought into being. The play's language affirms that determination to enlarge life: even at the end, Cleopatra speaks as woman, lover, and mother. After all, it is only by Roman tongues that the hero and heroine are spoken of as mere voluptuaries, softened and weakened by self-indulgence and excess. Antony's and Cleopatra's speech is consistently vigorous, various, copious, vivid, liveliest in those remarkable passages where excessive behavior, excessive sensation, excessive emotions are given their due.

Even though it threatens to do so, this hyperbolical play does not get out of hand: its images are as closely controlled as those of the other late tragedies. Further, the richness and decoration of the language, in passages of passionate disgust as in passages of grandiloquent elevation, match the richness of temperament which confers upon their characters the privilege of an equal elevation. What at first sounds like bombast in Antony's speech is naturalized in the course of the play, until his way of speaking becomes a standard against which other men are judged. Of effeminacy, slackness, or idleness, Antony's behavior may sometimes be accused—but never his language, nor Cleopatra's. From first to last what emerges is its affirmation of activity, of creativity, of unending and unendingly interesting emotional process. Till their very last breaths, these persons change and develop, to involve the audience in that development toward greatness. During the course of the play, then, Antony and Cleopatra grow into their rhetorical measure. At the play's start, Philo had called a spade a spade, or even a shovel; in contrast, Antony and Cleopatra spoke in love's arrogant, idealized overstatements. By the end of the play, Philo's linguistic practice is blocked out by Antony's hyperbole coming true, until we too believe that "the nobleness of life" is for such lovers to embrace. Until the very end, we are never quite sure of Cleopatra, such is the oscillation of the play and the woman between extremes, from rejection to reunion, from reviling to reaffirmation, from lie to truth, from denigration to encomium.

By their manner of dying, these figures are known: the Roman world, with all its real space, could not house the love of Antony for Cleopatra. That Antony lost his place in the real world, lost that world altogether, is made to seem unimportant beside the imaginative satisfactions of his emotional life. What Antony and Cleopatra do and say represents them: for all their own vacillation and oscillation, they turn out to be true in their ultimate commitment to each other. Antony dies with energy and (oddly enough) enthusiasm; Cleopatra looks to her last moment and beyond it, both on earth and in Elysium—she remains alive, feeling, imagining, to her last breath. Both catch and express their visions of the new heaven, new earth, seen always in terms of each other and of being with each other. They die as they had lived, beyond definition, in expectation of more. It is the strength, the vividness, the vigor of excess which this play presents, examines, criticizes, and ultimately, with full understanding, confirms, in a language of hyperbole built to match the size and scope of the subject. In the *ping* and *pong* of plain and grandiloquent styles, now one seeming to lead and now the other, Shakespeare manages to show us the problem and the problematics, in moral as in literary terms, at the heart of style. By sinking the notions associated with the Asiatic style back into life itself, in the play's dramatic action he can examine and assess both the style and the style of life in terms of each other, and to see them as one. He can demonstrate, then, by the peculiarly literary device of a stylistic agon, the moral problematics of dimension, can manage to make acceptable—more, to make admirable and comprehensible—the values of an honestly ostentatious style.

Mimesis and Modernity in *Antony and Cleopatra*

Howard Felperin

That *Antony and Cleopatra* creates an ambiguity of effect and response unprecedented even within Shakespeare's work is documented by a history of interpretation that wavers inconclusively between Egyptian and Roman viewpoints, and that usually feels compelled finally to side with one or the other position, however tentatively or tactfully. It is not immediately obvious, however, that the play's dominant ambiguity of effect arises from the juxtaposition of older and newer, allegorical and parodic, levels of action that we have been tracing as a constitutive feature of Shakespearean tragedy. On the contrary, does the play not present a pagan and classical world that manifestly exists outside native morality influences? Yet we need not even go as far back as the revenges of the Vice-like Aaron in *Titus Andronicus* to find Shakespeare changing his classical sources and subject matter into the currency of his own popular dramatic tradition. The machinations of the Vice and the machinery of revenge are still clearly visible in Cassius's temptation of Brutus and the appearance of Caesar's ghost within *Julius Caesar*. In *Antony and Cleopatra,* it is the principals themselves who attempt to impose, in characteristic Shakespearean fashion, a morality structure upon themselves and their world, a structure closely analogous to the by now familiar one adopted by Hal in the earlier moral history, *Henry IV, Part 1.*

For in *Antony and Cleopatra* too we see a worldly prince flanked

---

From *Shakespearean Representation: Mimesis and Modernity in Elizabethan Tragedy.* © 1977 by Princeton University Press.

by figures of vice and virtue and engaged in a movement toward redemption in which the former is reluctantly but inevitably cast off and the latter embraced. Indeed, the large structural contours of the play, as seen from the lovers', particularly Cleopatra's, viewpoint, could not be more transparently morality-derived. "O infinite virtue, com'st thou smiling from / The world's great snare uncaught" (4.8.17–18), she greets the temporarily victorious Antony, equating Caesar and the Romans with the temptations of the world, and herself and Egypt with a saving love. Obviously certain major adjustments and displacements have already been worked on the older vision of transcendence to enable the lovers to adopt it as their own. For one thing, the virtues of love and faith incarnated and preached by Cleopatra are hardly those of traditional Christian allegory; in her carnality and selfishness, she might well be said to embody the very opposite of Christian virtue, yet the play, as even its most Roman commentators have often pointed out, systematically transvalues her vices into virtues, for they partake of a quality of transcendence that is repeatedly said to be sacred and divine. Nor is the "salvation" the lovers finally see their way clear to in the end the traditional Christian one of the moralities. Their "marriage" is a shared figure of speech; their "afterlife" in a pastoral underworld an imaginative projection; Antony's apotheosis takes the form of the visual pun of being raised aloft on creaking pulleys. And all this is achieved by the most un-Christian means of a double suicide. Obviously the allegorical model to which the lovers would assimilate themselves and their experience is already something of a parody.

If this neo- or pseudo-morality structure were the only one, or even the major one, employed within the play, the effect would certainly be highly ambiguous, given the relatively loose fit and the amount of adjustment necessary between the present action and the prior model. But this initial ambiguity is increased almost geometrically by virtue of the fact that juxtaposed against the model employed by the lovers is another competing model of experience. For the Romans have adopted for their own purposes of self-mythologization the heroic model of the renaissance epic. Seen from within that literary convention, Cleopatra is no longer a figure of the saving power of love and grace, however displaced or redefined, but a figure of deceit and corruption, seducing the hero from his true mission of self-realization through heroic conquest. Cleopatra is assigned, through the Romans' language and imagery, a place within a long line of emasculating and hypererotic femmes fatales, stretching from the Venus, Omphale, Circe, and Dido of classical tradition to the Armida, Duessa, and Acrasia of more recent renaissance epics. Antony becomes the enfeebled descendant of Hercules figuratively as well as genealogically, and Octavius becomes the surviving heir to the line of antique virtue. This is the screen through which all the Romans, including Antony himself much of the time, view the experience of the play, from Philo's opening speech announcing "The triple pillar of the world transformed / Into a strumpet's fool" to Octavius's closing description of Cleopatra looking "As she would catch another Antony / In her strong toil of grace." Even Enobarbus's depiction of Cleopatra on Cydnus, usually quoted in support of her claim to transcendence, falls squarely within this renaissance epic and pictorial tradition in its emphasis on fine excess and analogy with the sexually threatening Venus. Of course this high epic tradition that the Romans invoke and cultivate throughout the play contains its own suggestion of parody. The latter-day embodiment of Herculean virtue, "scarce-bearded Caesar," has come down in the world considerably from his heroic antecedents, refusing on pragmatic grounds Antony's anachronistic challenge to single combat, and exhibiting throughout a politician's preference for the duplicities of the fox over the directness of the Nemean lion. Such ironies should at least prevent us from privileging the Roman view of things, as truer or closer to "reality," over that of the lovers. Both are equally fictive and equally at variance with their implied prototypes.

If these rival constructs were allowed to remain impenetrable to one another while alternately presenting contradictory images of character and action, the overall effect would be one not of ambiguity and ambivalence but of schizophrenia or solipsism, as it is in the closing scenes of *Troilus and Cressida.* But in *Antony and Cleopatra,* as Octavius's phrase "strong toil of grace" suggests, there is considerable interpenetration between its two rival constructs as they engage each other in a dialectic of mutual demystification. For each enables us to see the weakness or inadequacy of the other as a model of conduct. It is the Roman vision of the lovers as a pair of degenerate hedonists that reveals, against their own vision of themselves, how lacking in anything like a social morality is the neomorality they stage. If their vision were generally adopted, there could not be a society at all, much less an empire. Conversely, it is the lovers' vision of the Romans as a gang of petty worldlings that reveals, against their own self-mythologization, how far short of their epic forbears these squabbling and treacherous

Romans fall. Yet these rival constructs are simultaneously engaged in a dialectic of mutual remystification. By adopting an epic model, however short of its ideal of heroic magnanimity they themselves fall, the Romans enable us to see that the lovers' reconstituted virtue approaches this very epic norm. Similarly, the lovers' morality vision, though they have emptied it of conventional morality, enables us to see that this older-style morality, as embodied by Fulvia and Octavia, is the very pillar on which the Roman social order rests. Both older visions might actually seem to have survived their mutual conflict in Caesar's closing speech: "No grave upon the earth shall clip in 't / A pair so famous." Here the Romans' historical and rhetorical model of epic glory ("A pair so *famous*") has apparently been reconciled with the lovers' model of saving passion ("No grave shall *clip*"), since the spokesman of the former has adopted the vocabulary of the latter. The impression of reconciliation is only momentary, however, since Caesar's speech goes on to glorify himself and Rome in terms of their *triumph over* the lovers, whose story is "No less in pity than his glory which / Brought them to be lamented." Caesar does not so much adopt their language as commandeer it as the spoils of victory. Of course this is no more than what Antony and Cleopatra have already done in claiming to have validated their own transcendent vision of passion and "marriage" by committing suicide "in the high Roman manner." The apparent reconciliation of contending models in the end gives way to a continuing and endless process of demystification and remystification of older models we have seen to be characteristic of Shakespearean tragedy.

Though this interaction of older conventions does begin to imply or triangulate the reality of the lovers and their experience, it cannot, for all its richness and complexity, finally contain and comprehend those realities. We can believe that the lovers have indeed succeeded in defining themselves and validating their love in the terms they insist upon, if we wish, but to do so is to regard their and Shakespeare's art as a kind of displaced religion and to disregard Shakespeare's presentation of it as merely art. When Cleopatra, for example, at the play's most intense moment of theatrical self-consciousness imagines "Some squeaking Cleopatra boy my greatness / In the posture of a whore" (5.2.214–15), she appropriates the terms of the Roman vision of her only to disclaim them. She is not, she implies, this caricature of a whore the Romans would make her out to be. She parodies their parody, deconstructs their construct of disapproval and doubt, rendering it null and void. This opens up imaginative space for her own "immortal longings" to express themselves, for her to become once again and once and for all an allegorical being of "fire and air, / My baser elements I give to baser life." But how can we simply lay aside our awareness that her greatness *is* being "boyed" and perhaps even "squeaked" in something very like the posture of a whore by the boy-actor playing her, at least in Elizabethan production, and at the very moment such artistic mockery is disclaimed and supposedly transcended to make way for authentic reality? Or when Antony asserts "I am Antony still," there is no more basis for identifying him with the walking hyperbole that defines Antony within Cleopatra's vision than with the reeling reduction of a "strumpet's fool" that defines him within the Romans'. The play cannot finally bring moral resolution out of what remains a double image, but it is precisely in its moral irresolution that its mimetic fidelity consists. The failure of their efforts toward self-deification is what defines them in their exemplary humanity.

Like Shakespeare's earlier tragedies, *Antony and Cleopatra* can finally only point toward, but cannot present, a stable selfhood that resides beneath the roles adapted from the repertory of literary and dramatic tradition, a reality that does not vary like the shore of the great world or dislimn like the cloud-rack. But this reality cannot exist as such within the play, and remains just beyond the reach, though not the reference, of its own art. Unlike *Lear* and the earlier tragedies, however, *Antony and Cleopatra* does not end in intense aporia, but only because the lovers, and the Romans, accept as true the rhetoric of their own models, as Lear and the other tragic heroes can never quite do. In this respect, the play moves toward the joyful reunion with its implied models that characterizes Shakespearean comedy and romance rather than toward the unsettling divergence that characterizes Shakespearean tragedy. This feeling may well be what moved A. C. Bradley to remark that "for a tragedy it is not painful" and what has led many others to think of the play as somehow different from the four great tragedies and to be discussed in different terms. But the fact remains that Shakespeare has at every point made it possible to resist this movement of the play toward convergence with either or both its inscribed models, if only because those models are mutually contradictory to the end, which is also what finally maintains the play within the mode of tragedy. Sidney's fundamental insight that "the poet never lieth because he nothing affirmeth" fits no poet better than the Shakespeare of the tragedies, including the Shakespeare of *Antony and Cleopatra*.

Determined Things: The Case of *Antony and Cleopatra*

John Bayley

Antony and Cleopatra is in the simplest sense the most determined of all Shakespeare's tragic plays. The consciousness tragedies are by contrast areas of infinite possibility: menace, relief, the untoward, and the unlooked-for saving and mercy—all seem possible or imminent. In *King Lear* the question of fatality does not even arise: neither the expected nor the unexpected has any relevance in terms of the family situation it involves us in. But in *Antony and Cleopatra* and in different ways and degrees in *Coriolanus* and *Timon,* the notion of fatality is wholly dominant. There is nothing overpowering about it; it is not the *moira* of ancient Greek tragedy, the force which even the gods are helpless to control and which is constantly invoked by choruses with awe and resignation. Nor does it in any way resemble the *Schicksal* of German Romantic drama, a melodramatic affair which parodies the classical realisation and turns it into a kind of luxury of doom. Fate in this sense is also a flamboyant presence in Jacobean drama, personified by hero, villain or revenger: "Canst thou weep fate from his determined purpose?—so soon wilt thou weep me." In Shakespeare's tragedies of consciousness the conceptualising of fate, stylised in the equivocation of the prophesying witches who deceive Macbeth, is never situated inside consciousness itself. When Othello exclaims, "Who can control his fate?" it seems like an afterthought, a recollection of how the situation he is in might be described from outside, and in the perspective of literary experience.

From *Shakespeare and Tragedy.* © 1981 by John Bayley. Routledge & Kegan Paul, 1981.

But fate in *Antony and Cleopatra* has something almost good-natured about it, relaxed and familiar. The tone of the poetry, simultaneously terse and expansive, easy and strenuous, reinforces this impression. To give way to what is coming is the proper rule of life, most memorably expressed by Octavius Caesar himself:

> Cheer your heart!
> Be you not troubled with the time, which drives
> O'er your content these strong necessities;
> But let determined things to destiny
> Hold unbewailed their way.
>
> (3.6.81–85)

Such is the advice that Caesar gives his sister Octavia, and its tone is very like the "advice" that floats before Antony's eyes in the form of the image of the "cloud that's dragonish." It seems not a stoical precept but an invitation to repose and tranquillity. Fate in this play comes in the image of the baby at the breast "that sucks the nurse asleep." It was the sentiment of this perhaps, as much as anything, that made Bradley feel that, in spite of "a triumph which is more than reconciliation," there is something "disenchanting" in the tragic story, which does not move us as do the love dramas of Romeo or of Othello. "And the fact that we mourn so little saddens us."

But the audience yields to the story in the same spirit as the participants. Relaxation goes deeper than Bradley's impression would suggest. Constantly the poetry ties itself into a tight knot that suddenly comes loose, the strands slackening apart from each other.

> The wife of Antony
> Should have an army for an usher, and
> The neighs of horses to tell of her approach
> Long ere she did appear. The trees by the way
> Should have borne men; and expectation fainted,
> Longing for what it had not. Nay, the dust
> Should have ascended to the roof of heaven,
> Raised by your populous troops. But you are come
> A market-maid to Rome.
>
> (3.6.43–51)

There are two things to notice about this passage. The phrase about "expectation" recalls similar verbal effects, like the fans in Enobarbus's account of the scene at Cydnus, which "what they undid, did," and the air that went to gaze on Cleopatra and left a gap in nature. More important, the end of all the to-ing and fro-ing is the appearance of Octavia as a simple market-maid, as Cleopatra herself becomes

> No more but e'en a woman, and commanded
> By such poor passion as the maid that milks
> And does the meanest chares.
>
> (4.15.73–75)

Efforts, like language, relax their strain and drop into simplicity, "lie down and stray no farther," which is very different from the hero's rest at the end of tragic actions that have laboured to attain the hour. It is important that the sense of surrender, the drop from achievement into indifference, can come at any point in the play: it is not a gradual and cumulative process. Antony is the bellows and the fan at the beginning of the action, a phrase that though it undoubtedly means two types of cooling instrument—Shakespeare's frequent stylistic trick of putting two synonyms together—nonetheless suggests a to-and-fro, negative and positive indefinitely repeated, like the image of the fans that both cool and inflame Cleopatra's cheeks. The whole effect is one of sexual rise and fall, endorsing and yet also ironically contradicting the admiration of Cleopatra as making hungry where most she satisfies. In her last speeches Cleopatra herself calls up the idea in a concealed sexual reference—she must make haste and follow Antony, for otherwise Iras may meet him and he "will make demand of her and spend that kiss which is my heaven to have." The word "spend" tells its own tale: Antony has spent himself in this homely fashion many a time throughout the play.

Oscillation—the "swan's down feather" and the "vagabond flag" upon the stream—fills the action, though interestingly it applies neither to Octavius Caesar nor to Cleopatra herself. It is Octavia who, as Antony tenderly says, shows it when she parts from her brother, looking both towards him and towards her new husband:

> Her tongue will not obey her heart, nor can
> Her heart inform her tongue: the swan's down feather,
> That stands upon the swell at the full of tide
> And neither way inclines.
>
> (3.2.47–50)

The current of the play is indeed tidal, bearing those who are at its disposal forward and backward. Octavius is not like that, and he speaks contemptuously of those that are:

> This common body
> Like to a vagabond flag upon the stream
> Goes to and back, lack'ying the varying tide,
> To rot itself with motion.
>
> (1.4.44–47)

Octavia's hesitation is the same helplessness at a higher level—hers the down feather to the water-flag of the populace—and though her brother loves her he makes use of her, as of all others. But the action makes a silent distinction between the power to feel emotion and the state of helpless feeling. Octavius is no cold hypocrite, and the tears he weeps as he parts from his sister are not crocodile tears. In their little aside together Enobarbus and Agrippa make the point that both Antony and Octavius are men of tears, and it is clear that this is not what makes them different. Octavius's emotions simply accompany his will, while those of Antony agitate him without progression, "like to the time o' th' year between the extremes / Of hot and cold."

The structure of the play, then, expresses itself in the general helplessness of external and exterior life, willy-nilly subject to the alternation of action and passivity. Nothing less tragic in the usual sense can be imagined, as Bradley clearly felt, but there is no usual sense in which Shakespeare is tragic: the joys and fatigues of princely living, as they appear in a story of dying, are as appropriate a subject as the fall of princes. It is odd that Antony should come closest of any Shakespearean character to having what writers like Virginia Woolf have made us think of as a "stream of consciousness," which is clearly a very different thing from what appears in those tragedies of consciousness, *Hamlet, Othello,* and *Macbeth.* Antony is hurried, as Virginia Woolf felt was the fate of consciousness, from one impression and reaction to another; sensations and events fall on him: his death sequence itself is a rich and confused accumulation of them. This appears in a most striking way in the syntax of the passage after Antony has talked with the Soothsayer and then dismissed him to find the officer Ventidius:

> He shall to Parthia. Be it art or hap,
> He hath spoken true. The very dice obey him.
>
> (2.3.33–34)

The sense of consciousness vaguely flitting between one objective and another is as graphic here as it is with Mrs Dalloway or Mrs Bloom, and is expressed in the three different references of the same pronoun. *He* is Ventidius, also the Soothsayer, also Octavius. Dramatic inflection and pause would easily distinguish them, but Antony's awareness of things manufactures frustration and helplessness rather than distinctions, the decision which ends the speech seems a mere symptom of the vagaries of that awareness and its brooding in the toils of incongruous detail:

> His cocks do win the battle still of mine
> When it is all to naught, and his quails ever
> Beat mine, inhooped, at odds. I will to Egypt.
>
> (2.3.37–39)

The sentence in Plutarch which clearly gave Shakespeare the clue for his treatment of Antony relates to the way in which Cleopatra had secretly bribed Canidius, Antony's general and commander of the landforces, to recommend her remaining at advanced H.Q., as her withdrawal might demoralise the Egyptian fleet, a formidable and necessary part of Antony's total armament. "For it was predestined," says Plutarch, "that the government of all the world should fall into Octavius Caesar's hands." The passive sense of determined things, so foreign to every other tragedy, finds imaginative expression in *Antony and Cleopatra* through the nature of the hero's consciousness. He makes no effort to "take a bond of fate" or bid it, as Macbeth does, come into the lists and champion him to the utterance. Antony's mind acquiesces in what befalls him in the same way that the passive consciousness surrenders itself to passing experience, and it is incapable of that concentration and reflection that gives their individuality to Hamlet, Othello, and Macbeth. He evades such concentration as he here evades Caesar: and the incongruity between the lost games in a cock-or quail-pit, and the sudden impulse to set out for Egypt, indicate the process.

"No character is very strongly discriminated," observes Dr. Johnson of the play. Fate here seems to have leached out the kinds of individuality we are elsewhere accustomed to. Antony can only evade Caesar or be exasperated by him and dare him to personal combat, and again we are reminded of Cassius's way of escaping the elder Caesar's tyranny. But Cassius and Brutus, though their soldiership was not a patch on Antony's, seemed always to have an even chance of winning, a chance determined from the play's point of view by their whole mode of being and thinking. They are proper persons for conventional tragedy, working out their lot, heroically exposed to the shot of accident and dart of chance and the fatal misunderstanding which causes Cassius's suicide, in which his final words have all the recognition of appropriateness: "Caesar, thou art revenged, / Even with the sword that killed thee."

The lack of discrimination that Johnson noted is caused by two things—the mental processes in Antony and the lack of them in Caesar and in Cleopatra. Antony is unique in Shakespearean tragedy in being a lost man from the very beginning. The sense "of what he has, and has not," is as emphatic in the first scene as it is in his demeanour before the final battle. The ominous precedent is that of Pompey the Great, in his dishonoured grave by the sands of Alexandria, driven to his death by the inflexible will and luck of the first Caesar. Cleopatra recalls him as she muses on her conquests when Antony is away:

> Great Pompey
> Would stand and make his eyes grow in my brow:
> There he would anchor his aspect, and die
> With looking on his life.
>
> (1.5.31–34)

The same doomed paralysis is now to be continuously presented in Antony, but it gives us no sense of participation; no more does its opposite, the unmoved Caesar and the equally unmoved Cleopatra. Antony's self in the play engages with neither of them, and for the same reason, that both have such complete confidence in themselves and where they are going. One of the tactics of the piece is the simplification of Cleopatra, by a process that is analogous to the simplification of both Caesars. In all three cases Shakespeare abandons the indications of "wheels within wheels" in the source, and forgoes the political dimension which it indicates. There is no depth in defence here, no jockeying for position.

For in reality Antony was involved in a complicated political power-game with his rival and his mistress, and Plutarch thoroughly enjoyed revealing the ins and outs so far as he had got wind of them or could embroider on what he had heard. He too is of course turning events into story and illustration. Cleopatra was for Antony a powerful political ally in his attempts to gain hegemony over the whole

Middle East, an attempt that even before the breakup of the triumvirate had not been entirely successful. It was not only personally congenial to him but a part of Antony's political manoeuvring to "go native," a move which though it made him popular in the East compromised his reputation in Rome and Italy. Shakespeare of course ignores such success as he had: what must have struck the playwright's imagination was the way in which the hero's luck had turned. Even the loyalty of Octavia to himself and his family became a political liability, because her dignity and forbearance could not but make excellent propaganda for the Roman side: a consequence on which her brother had no doubt calculated.

Cleopatra, for her part, had put her money on Antony as the best bet not only to retain her kingdom but to further her ambition to become mistress of the Middle East. Her decision to accompany Antony on the Actium campaign, which Shakespeare artfully transmutes into the eternally vacuous wilfulness of the eternal feminine, was in reality a preemptive move to ensure that her colleague did not do a deal of his own with Octavius, leaving her out. The treachery and defection of client kings which Antony's Eastern policies had already set in train, was no doubt her fault as much as his, but no more. Though his narrative purposes required him to show how Antony was ruined by Cleopatra and his love for her, Plutarch's narration also reveals them in the clearest fashion as *colleagues*. And colleagues they remained, even in their last days, which in Plutarch's account have something pretentious and repellent about them, as well as sinister, for such episodes occurred as the handing over of Seleucus's wife and children to Antony for torture and death. Seleucus was commandant of the frontier fortress of Pelusium, and Cleopatra committed this deed in order to clear herself of suspicion when the town fell easily to the forces of Octavius Caesar. Shakespeare gives the name to the comic treasurer, who gives her away when she makes a declaration of her assets to Caesar, and he smilingly reassures her: "Nay, blush not, Cleopatra. I approve / Your wisdom in the deed."

That seems indeed the extent of Cleopatra's "naughtiness" in her comedy role. The change, and its significance, are clear. Cleopatra is to be as unremitting in her frivolity as Caesar in his pursuit of power. Between these two blank walls Antony's consciousness drifts to and fro. He can make nothing of them, and impose himself upon neither of them. And this pattern of course determines the general drift and image of the play. The hero is helpless in a unique sense, not like the conditions of any other tragedy.

The second clue which Shakespeare may have taken in his creative imagination of this process is Plutarch's comment on Antony's marriage in his young days, when he was a dissolute favourite of the older Caesar, to Fulvia. Plutarch remarks that in order to exercise self-control over his rackety existence Antony needed the help of a woman of character and strong personality.

> A woman not so basely minded to spend her time in spinning and housewifery, and was not contented to master her husband at home, but would also rule him in his office abroad, and command him that commanded legions and great armies; so that Cleopatra was to give Fulvia thanks that she had taught Antonius this obedience to women, that learned so well to be at their commandment.

Fulvia no doubt made a man of him in some sense, and loved him, for with the help of his brother she did her best to start a civil war in Italy to bring him home. But Cleopatra is a very different sort of woman. She may think herself powerful, and may have appealed to Antony because she seemed so, but in Shakespeare's presentation she is nothing of the sort. She demands attention; she affects authority and purpose; but really, and in her own robust way, she clings and vapours. She loves games and dreams and dressing up, and Antony's past makes him here the most congenial of playfellows. Their deep affection and love for each other here is undoubted, but she is not the woman to inspire him to action, as Fulvia was. Plutarch portrays her as a worthy successor to Fulvia, an enterprising if not altogether trustworthy colleague and comrade; but Shakespeare makes her a wholly different woman, not at all the sort that we may guess Fulvia to have been.

It is a part of Antony's helplessness that he never seems quite to find this out. She teases him, exasperates him, but fascinates him because he will go on against all the evidence in believing her to be stronger than he is. Her "strength" is like Octavius's "luck"—an impalpable thing whose influence is fateful to Antony because he so implicitly believes in it. If he is with her she is happy, and it matters not what is going on—peace or war. The latter seems to her a special sort of dressing up. "I'll give thee, friend, an armour all of gold: it was a king's," she tells Scarus, after Antony has praised his conduct in the last battle. She buckles on Antony's armour for him and he praises her: "Thou fumblest, Eros, and my queen's a squire / More tight at this than thou." This final desperate contest, nothing more than a forlorn gesture against an overwhelmingly strong and prudent enemy, seems in its excitement and innocence just like their Alexandrian revels, their inquisitive wanderings through the night streets together, the joke with the salt-fish on the hook which Antony "with fervency drew up."

Shakespeare has of course introduced a degree of romantic simplification and stylisation here which is in keeping with the taste of the age. Samuel Daniel had portrayed a very similar Cleopatra in his tragedy of 1594, and Dryden in *All for Love* was to take the hint from Shakespeare and give a total passivity and helplessness to both lovers. Mars and Venus, the conventions of tapestry and emblem, are convenient to the change, and exercise a traditional influence in the scene. But behind it is our sense of the woman herself, and the presentation of her as fatal for Antony in a touching and homely sense. Shakespeare joins on romantic preconceptions of the part to his portrait of a weak woman with a strong personality. Such a woman could not be—as Plutarch's Cleopatra is—in constant communication with Caesar behind Antony's back: when Thidias (Thyreus in Plutarch) comes to treat with her, she behaves with a genuinely girlish naivety, gratified to flirtatiousness by his courtesies, and professing respectful submission to his master. Neither means anything at all; they are merely symptoms of her instant, effortless way of dealing with every situation by being herself; the impression she gives is one of unbounded equanimity, whether she is giving audience to Caesar's representatives, mourning the fate of Antony, or ordering the asps *sotto voce* from Charmian while saying of Caesar; "He words me, girls, he words me."

Shakespeare's sense of omission, and of timing, is perfect to this presentation of her. This Cleopatra could not be mentioned as experimenting on prisoners to see which death was the easiest, though we don't in the least mind hearing after her death that "She hath pursued conclusions infinite / Of easy ways to die." Nor could she have joined in the intellectuals' pact, mentioned by Plutarch as the *Synapothanumenon*—"the order and agreement of those that are to die together"—which she and Antony used to celebrate in the last days with their friends. Our Cleopatra is no bluestocking, and neither coldhearted nor methodical. Oddly enough the touch in Plutarch that Shakespeare would normally have delighted to use, and whose incongruity would not in the least have disturbed her self-possession, is that the soldier to whom she gave the golden armour, "when he had received this rich gift, stole away by night and went to Caesar."

The most moving thing about their relation is the sense of two people, who have, in the misfortunes they bring on each other, become inextricably close. It is a closeness easily ruptured, as so many knots of style are easily dissolved in the play, and death itself seems gentler and easier for being prolonged, the "knot intrinsicate of life" insensibly untied. But the lovers are close rather than intimate. It is the only subtlety that can survive in their relationship, changed as it is from the sexual and professional intimacy of lovers and colleagues to Shakespeare's representation of the eternal feminine bewitching the grand captain, the greatest prince in the world. It is the only subtlety, I should say, that survives in the portrayal of the relationship, the most famous but also the most public love spectacle, not only in Shakespeare but anywhere in literature. The lovers are never alone together and there is no invitation to us to imagine them alone.

The role of Enobarbus, who hardly appears in Plutarch, is crucial here. Dramatically he is the confidant, unique in being the confidant of both lovers, as well as the candid friend and salty commentator. Typically, the role of confidant is naturalised by Shakespeare to the point where we feel that both lovers really do need him to inquire and consult with about each other. At the outset the matter is plainly put by Enobarbus, who is not, like most clever and cynical bystanders, seeing through the situation, but stating that there is no situation to see through:

ANTONY. She is cunning past man's thought.
ENOBARBUS. Alack, sir, no. Her passions are made of noth-
    ing but the finest part of pure love. We cannot call her
    winds and waters sighs and tears: they are greater
    storms and tempests than almanacs can report. This can-
    not be cunning in her: if it be she makes a shower of
    rain as well as Jove.
ANTONY. Would I had never seen her!
ENOBARBUS. O, sir, you had then left unseen a wonderful
    piece of work, which not to have been blest withal
    would have discredited your travel.

                                       (1.3.141ff.)

"*Alack, sir, no . . . .*" That is just the trouble. If she were cunning past man's thought, as her original may well have been, and as in a distant and unamiable fashion she appears in Plutarch's account, there would, in one sense, be no problem. Antony would still be overcome by Caesar, but he would be overcome making use of her, and being used by her. Her not being cunning makes for the innocence and openness of their love that transforms the play. The play is what it is, and not like any other, because of this.

Dramatically, a cunning Cleopatra who redeemed herself in Antony's last days, coming to love him absolutely in his defeat and their *liebestod,* would be effective but also banal. Shakespeare was in any case no doubt content to give his audience the traditional figure they expected, the love's martyr of Chaucer and Gower and Garnier's *Marc Antoine,* which Sir Philip Sidney's sister had translated. What he added was his own kind of simplicity, which echoes the simplicity— and the tradition—in the handling of the two great Caesars. The presentment of them all is absolute and on the surface: there is nothing to find behind it. But the sublime simplicity of Cleopatra has its inimitable Shakespearean quality, and as we should expect it is that of the comedy sublime. At the beginning of the Actium campaign we have the perfect example of it. Antony is discussing with his general the reports of Caesar's swift progress:

> ANTONY.   Is it not strange, Canidius,
>   That from Tarentum and Brundusium
>   He could so quickly cut the Ionian sea
>   And take in Toryne? You have heard on't sweet?
> CLEOPATRA. Celerity is never more admired
>   Than by the negligent.
>
> (3.7.20–25)

The intended put-down of that reply, its silliness and its self-possession, is impenetrable. An actress like Joyce Grenfell might do it justice, but she would not be able to play a straight Cleopatra, for Cleopatra never gives the faintest hint of parodying herself. If it were so she might indeed be cunning. The scene, just before Actium, is one of the most brilliant and compact in the whole play, opening with Cleopatra and Enobarbus alone together:

> CLEOPATRA. I will be even with thee, doubt it not.
> ENOBARBUS. But why, why, why?

> CLEOPATRA. Thou has forspoke my being in these wars,
>   And sayst it is not fit.
> ENOBARBUS.   Well, is it, is it?

Enobarbus's exasperation, with its despairing repetitions, is an open and comic outcry of the powerlessness that Antony feels before both Cleopatra and Caesar. Critics have suggested that Shakespeare is inconsistent through his usual rapidity (or carelessness) and concentration on the scene rather than the play. Here is the politically steely Cleopatra who does not appear elsewhere? But surely Shakespeare has deftly substituted a Cleopatra determined not to leave Antony for a Plutarchan one who couldn't afford to let him out of her sight. The idea that the queen and her maids "manage this war" is absurd, as everybody knows it to be, including Cleopatra herself: that is the point of her observation about celerity. It shows what a card she is, a "great fairy"—it is just the sort of remark that Cleopatra *would* make. Her presence, we might note, divests every scene she is in of military and manlike seriousness: contrast with these scenes the ones—no less supple and brilliant—where Antony is alone in Italy with Caesar, Agrippa, Lepidus and the others. There the tone is genuinely businesslike—hard, watchful, courteous, dangerous. Antony there is holding his own in a real man's world.

Such a world of power is not of course any less inherently and humanly absurd than Cleopatra's world of feminine self-satisfaction. That is wonderfully suggested in the messenger's account of Antony's words for her, and when he spoke them:

> "All the east,
> Say thou, shall call her mistress." So he nodded,
> And soberly did mount an arm-gaunt steed,
> Which neighed so high that what I would have spoke
> Was beastly dumbed by him.
>
>   (1.5.46–50)

It has its animation, its triumphs and its poetry as well as the comedy which in Shakespeare is indivisible from these things, but it is basically as odious as the world of violence and intrigue must always be. The scene on board Pompey's galley, and the decency of its commander, does not obscure the fundamental truth of what he is tempted to do, and what his subsequent murder at the hands of the triumvirate shows he should have done.

But this realism does not extend to the later campaign scenes in which Cleopatra is present. There romance takes over, or rather the kind of feminine reality she represents, a reality none the less moving for being here shown as wholly powerless. All her influence can do is to remove any kind of represented seriousness from the concluding acts and battles. The skirmish outside Alexandria is portrayed in the play as a last chance to recoup Antony's fortunes. In fact it was nothing of the sort, a truth the play tacitly acknowledges in the dressing up for the encounter and the banquet after it, as well as in Cleopatra's womanly yearnings over Antony's challenge of Caesar to single combat (a challenge which—to further compound our issue—he may well have made in historical fact). She does not manage the wars, but her attentions have indeed effectively demoralised those who do, and it is true that both in the play and the historical events behind it her mere existence has made it impossible for Antony to come to terms with Caesar.

It is her presence which makes it possible for this play to make a virtue out of the artificiality of having battles take place just off-stage: a battle in Cleopatra's vicinity automatically becomes a make-believe, depriving of any conviction the masculine ploys which the play attempts to represent. The business of battle is put on one side in a somewhat similar, if less grand and touching, way at the end of *Julius Caesar,* where the represented events at Philippi are transformed by parting and the emotions of friendship—the farewells of Brutus and Cassius, and the Roman friendship that can still be invoked between the conspirators, their victim, and his avengers.

"Here's sport indeed—how heavy weighs my lord?" This is the reality which dominates and transforms the ending of the play, the surrender of the whole issue to helplessness and childhood. The price paid by the play is the impression that the disasters and imminent death that bring the lovers so close are not quite real anyway, no more real in terms of the play's imagination than they are in the necessary artifice of enactment. For Plutarch as for Shakespeare a legend died with Antony, the god Hercules forsaking him in music by night; and, taking the hint, Shakespeare gives the play up to something like music, and its "strong toil of grace." The transforming comedy truth of Cleopatra as "no more but e'en a woman" takes over, folding in its arms both the hero and the heroine herself.

The departure of Enobarbus is significant here, for in spite of Antony's final explosion after his last ships join the enemy it brings the pair, as lovers, more helplessly together. "Is Antony or we in fault for this?" the queen has asked him at their last meeting alone, and the query is dazed and childlike in the same way as Antony's own query to his sardonic lieutenant a little later on, when Caesar has refused the challenge to single combat. " 'He will not fight with me, Domitius?' 'No.' 'Why should he not?' " It is the same note as the break in Antony's voice when he addresses her after the outburst of rage over Thidias—"Cold-hearted toward me?"—to which her reply is the warmest, most enfolding she has yet given him:

> Ah, dear, if it be so,
> From my cold heart let heaven engender hail.

To Antony's rhetorical indignation her reply has been "Not know me yet?"—a question in which there is nothing wise or fathomless. Antony has never known her because he has been so insistent on his image of her as all-powerful queen of love and serpent of old Nile. But in that sense there is nothing to know. The query is the reverse of the species of telling stroke in tragedy which suddenly reveals a psychological truth. Such are Lady Macbeth's "had he not resembled / My father as he slept." Hermione's cry to Oreste in Racine's *Andromaque*—"Qui te l'a dit?"—when he has slain on her orders the man she loved; Clytemnestra's grief when told the lie that her son, whom she knows will try to kill her, is dead. Such a stroke of truth is the reverse of anything that will happen in *Antony and Cleopatra*. What moves as its tragedy is that only in dying will the pair be close to one another, but then they will be close indeed. Their weakness blurs all distinctions and brings them, at last, into a deep intimacy with the audience. They are no longer social types, living in Plutarch's larger-than-life world of the powerful and great. Her rhetoric of death turns again to a child's game as she gives instructions to Charmian:

> when thou hast done this chare, I'll give thee leave
> To play till doomsday. Bring our crown and all.

And it is with a child's idea of comfort that she remembers Antony in death:

> As sweet as balm, as soft as air, as gentle—
> O Antony—[*To the asp*] Nay, I will take thee too:
> What should I stay.

She is asleep before she can finish the sentence. Charmian completes it for her, and straightens her up like a nurse removing a toy: "Your crown's awry. / I'll mend it, and then play." Fortune has followed them all, in its own way, throughout; as requested, the Soothsayer at the beginning told "but a workyday fortune." To be sleepy is the proper end to a working-day.

Gender and Genre

Linda Bamber

Cleopatra, says Enobarbus, is to be understood in terms of her "variety" (2.2.238). He means that she is a surprising person, that her moods are changeable and her personality many-sided. But Cleopatra is also various as an element in the drama. She is more than one kind of character, which may be why she provokes so much disagreement among critics. For my purposes there are three Cleopatras. At one level she is the embodiment of Egypt and a symbol of our antihistorical experience. At another level she represents the Other as against Antony's representation of the Self. As such, she appears indifferent to the destiny of the male Self; here, as in the other Shakespearean tragedies, the hero's encounter with this apparently indifferent Other is an important part of his tragic-heroic adventure. And finally Cleopatra is a character like Antony himself, facing failure and defeat, motivated by the desire to contain or rise above her losses. Let us begin with the first and most familiar Cleopatra, Cleopatra-as-Egypt.

This first Cleopatra is an alternative, for the reader and for Antony, to Caesar and Rome. She has had the lion's share of the critical attention, so it is unnecessary to deal with her at great length. This Cleopatra is the "serpent of old Nile" (1.5.25), a principle of pleasure, of fertility and decay, of artifice, of ambiguity. She opposes the cold, abstract certainties of Rome with the heat of her body; Caesar chal-

From *Comic Women, Tragic Men: A Study of Gender and Genre in Shakespeare.* © 1982 by the Board of Trustees of the Leland Stanford Junior University. Stanford University Press, 1982.

lenges Antony to be preeminent in the world of men whereas Cleopatra challenges him to his destiny as a lover. She represents the Egypt Antony describes to Lepidus when he returns to Rome:

> The higher Nilus swells,
> The more it promises; as it ebbs, the seedsman
> Upon the slime and ooze scatters his grain,
> And shortly comes to harvest.
>
> (2.7.21–24)

This Cleopatra is not so much a character in her own right as an experience of Antony's and a problem for his judgment. This is the one who might be good or bad, who attacks and eludes both the audience and the hero. Is she finally faithful to Antony or not? Is it worth giving up the honors of Rome to pursue something so shifty and unpossessable? We can never know. Take, for instance, the scene in which Cleopatra apparently plans to defect to Caesar. Thidias tells Cleopatra that Caesar "knows you embraced not Antony / As you did love, but as you feared him," and Cleopatra, as soon as she can collect her wits, responds, "He is a god, and knows / What is most right" (3.13.56–57, 60–61). This is enough for Enobarbus, who leaves to tell Antony that Cleopatra is "quitting" him. But Enobarbus only witnesses this speech in the first place because Cleopatra insists that he stay to hear it. Is it possible that Cleopatra *means* Enobarbus to report her to Antony? Could this be merely another ploy for Antony's attention and not really a betrayal? Furthermore, the scene ends with Enobarbus's desertion, not Cleopatra's: "I will seek," says Enobarbus, "Some way to leave him" (3.13.200–201). So we must ask ourselves, in retrospect, who was being faithful to Antony here, Enobarbus or Cleopatra? He actually does leave Antony (although he later returns in spirit) whereas she does not (or does she?). To hunt for this Cleopatra is to double back so many times that we forget what we were looking for. As Egypt, Cleopatra is radically ambiguous and can never be finally known.

The Cleopatra Antony perceives is this elusive one. He cannot wholly love her or wholly leave her; he can never bring himself to make final judgments of her, and yet he cannot put judgment aside. Only when he believes she is dead or when he is himself dying can he act from a love unmixed with fear and suspicion. Antony's fears are for his place in history as well as for the returns on his love. He has trusted his reputation to Cleopatra; if she is untrue to him, his fate will have been that of a strumpet's fool. He dies with his essential question about her unanswered, although at the moment of his death he is no longer interested in such questions.

If we read Cleopatra entirely as a principle, *our* question about her goes unanswered also. We do not know whether she is good or bad, important or trivial, Antony's greatest adventure or his "dotage" (1.1.1). John Danby is one of many critics who read Cleopatra as Egypt; his excellent essay on *Antony and Cleopatra* quite explicitly recognizes the consequences of doing so. That is, his essay deals with what *I* consider the consequences of doing so; Danby himself does not connect what I see as interpretive cause and effect. If Cleopatra is Egypt and the crucial dialectic is between Egypt and Rome, the play does not resolve, does not progress, does not reach any kind of tragic climax. Neither Egypt nor Rome represents values endorsed by the play as a whole:

> The Roman condemnation of the lovers is obviously inadequate. The sentimental reaction in their favor is equally mistaken. There is no so-called "love-romanticism" in the play. The flesh has its glory and its passion, its witchery. Love in *Antony and Cleopatra* is both these. The love of Antony and Cleopatra, however, is not asserted as a "final value". . . . To . . . claim that there is a "redemption" motif in Antony and Cleopatra's love is an . . . error. To the Shakespeare who wrote *King Lear* it would surely smack of blasphemy. The fourth and fifth acts of *Antony and Cleopatra* are not epiphanies. They are the ends moved to by that process whereby things rot themselves with motion—unhappy and bedizened and sordid, streaked with the mean, the ignoble, the contemptible. . . .
>
> *Antony and Cleopatra* is an account of things in terms of the World and the Flesh, Rome and Egypt, the two great contraries that maintain and destroy each other, considered apart from any third sphere which might stand over against them.
>
> (John Danby, *Poets on Fortune's Hill*)

King Lear, according to Danby, is eschatological, *Antony and Cleopatra* merely analytical. In the latter play opposite temperaments are merely weighed against each other, and each is found wanting the others virtues. There is a "diminution of scope" from the earlier tragedies.

What is missing from *Antony and Cleopatra,* according to Danby, is the theme of "Nature." By "Nature" he means "a reality that transcends the political and the personal," something that tests the soul of man. King Lear, says Danby, is tested and tempered by Nature, by the world beyond the Self; the characters in *Antony and Cleopatra* test only each other, commenting on each other's limitations. So *"Antony and Cleopatra* gives the impression of being a technical tour-de-force which Shakespeare enjoyed for its own sake."

Danby's Nature seems very close to what I have been calling the Other: a reality external to the Self with which the hero is confronted in tragedy. We do battle with this Other because it seems to betray us, to make us less than we were; ultimately we transcend our antagonism to it, at which point it no longer seems implacably hostile to us. The dialectic between the Self and the Other, often reflected in the dialectical progression of the hero's relationship with women, does seem to resolve in tragedy. This dialectic—unlike the dialectic Danby finds between Egypt and Rome—does not simply exhaust itself. It creates something new: the tragic hero in his final phase, the Self transformed. If we read Cleopatra as the representative of the Other and not merely as Egypt, the diachronic movement of the play, which Danby sees as wholly "discreating," takes on a more positive aspect.

In a sense, of course, there is little difference between Cleopatra as Egypt and Cleopatra as the Other, for it is *as* Egypt that Cleopatra represents the Other. But in this reading Egypt and Rome are no longer equal but opposite options for the hero. In this reading Egypt is the new world, the world that calls into question all the old certainties, the heath on which Antony faces the indifference of the universe and his own falling off from what he means to be. Egypt replaces or rewrites Rome as experience replaces and rewrites innocence. When Antony returns to Rome, it is gone; the world in which physical courage and manly purpose prevail has been replaced by a world of drinking, matchmaking, speechifying, and deal-making. Roman honor, after Antony's time in Egypt, has become as elusive and dubious an ideal as Egyptian love. What it *had been* we may gather from Caesar's description of Antony before Egypt, on campaign:

> Antony,
> Leave thy lascivious wassails. When thou once
> Was beaten from Modena, where thou slew'st
> Hirtius and Pansa, consuls, at thy heel

Did famine follow, whom thou fought'st against
(Though daintily brought up) with patience more
Than savages could suffer. Thou didst drink
The stale of horses and the gilded puddle
Which beasts would cough at. Thy palate then did deign
The roughest berry on the rudest hedge.
Yea, like the stag when snow the pasture sheets,
The barks of trees thou browsed. On the Alps
It is reported thou didst eat strange flesh,
Which some did die to look on. And all this
(It wounds thine honor that I speak it now)
Was borne so like a soldier that thy cheek
So much as lanked not.

(1.4.55–71)

Prelapsarian Rome, like all the prelapsarian worlds of Shakespearean tragedy, was a world in which honor and manhood followed directly from the fulfillment of clear-cut criteria. In returning to Rome Antony means to return to a more clearly defined manhood; he means to return to his old role as a fighting general. "The beds i' th' East are soft," he tells Pompey,

and thanks to you,
That called me timelier than my purpose hither;
For I have gained by't.

(2.6.50–52)

But Rome can no longer be represented by the hardened body of the general on campaign. In its own way it has gone as soft as the beds in the East; it is pictured as a mean and drunken party on a boat. After Egypt the corruption of Rome is revealed, to Antony and to us. Antony's return to Egypt is inevitable; the old world is gone and he has no choice but to live in the new.

If Egypt, then, is the new world—the world of the Other and not merely an equal-but-opposite alternative to Rome—then Cleopatra's identification with Egypt offers us the possibility of a different interpretation from Danby's. In this case we may interpret the phases of Antony's relationship to Cleopatra as phases in his response to the new world. Seen from this point of view, the play seems less committed than Danby thinks to "the sense of ripe-rottenness and hopelessness, the vision of self-destruction [and] the feeling of . . . fevered futility."

Danby charts the falling curve of the dialectic between Egypt and Rome; this dialectic, as he points out, loses energy as the play goes on. But the dialectic between Self and Other gains energy until it reaches a kind of resolution. The second dialectic begins with the refusal of the Other, develops into misogynist rage, and resolves into kindness and connectedness.

It may seem paradoxical to refer to Antony's early relations with Cleopatra as a species of denial. His first speech, after all, is one of the most famous declarations of love in all of literature:

> Let Rome in Tiber melt, and the wide arch
> Of the ranged empire fall! Here is my space,
> Kingdoms are clay: our dungy earth alike
> Feeds beast as man. The nobleness of life
> Is to do thus; when such a mutual pair
> And such a twain can do't, in which I bind,
> On pain of punishment, the world to weet
> We stand up peerless.
>
> (1.1.33–40)

But from this point until his reunion with Cleopatra in act 3, scene 7, Antony fights a losing battle to limit his relationship with her, to avoid the choice he so grandly claims, in the first scene, already to have made. He succumbs to the Roman view of his relationship, returns to Rome and marries Octavia. Antony does not deny his desire for Cleopatra; but he denies the revolutionary nature of his desire. He denies the radical changes in the Self that will be necessary to accommodate the Other; he denies the choice she imposes between Rome and Egypt, between an asexual and a sexual identity. Rome, of course, is opposed to sexuality not per se but only as it interferes with business. Caesar defines the Roman position as follows:

> Let's grant it is not
> Amiss to tumble on the bed of Ptolemy
>
> . . . .
>
> . . . yet must Antony
> No way excuse his foils when we do bear
> So great weight in his lightness. If he filled
> His vacancy with his voluptuousness,
> Full surfeits and the dryness of his bones
> Call on him for't. But to confound such time

That drums him from his sport and speaks as loud
As his own state and ours, 'tis to be chid
As we rate boys who, being mature in knowledge
Pawn their experience to the present pleasure
And so rebel to judgment.

(1.4.16–17, 23–33)

To Caesar and Rome, relationships with women are a leisure-time activity, something to fill up "vacancy." When serious business is broached—war or political realignments or the dividing up of land—a man who continues to "tumble on the bed" risks his place in the world of men. A sexual adventure is a luxury, an excursion one might make from a journey whose goals lie elsewhere. Antony's very decision to return to Cleopatra reflects the Roman attitude toward sexuality: "I will to Egypt," Antony says, "And though I make this marriage for my peace, / I' th' East my pleasure lies" (2.3.37–39). The imperial Self visits here and there, demanding "peace" in one place and "pleasure" in another. The Other is denied its dialectical relationship with the Self and valued only insofar as it brings pleasure. In this phase of the drama the Self refuses the Other and puts his faith in the firmness of his own boundaries.

Antony's first action of the play is his departure from Egypt. We are not really sorry to see him leave; we are pleased to see him recover his decisiveness and resist Cleopatra's wiles. But we should be troubled, I think, to notice that Antony's language as he leaves for Rome becomes transparently rhetorical. "By the fire / That quickens Nilus' slime," he tells Cleopatra,

> I go from hence
> Thy soldier-servant, making peace or war
> As thou affects.

(1.3.68–71)

This is simply untrue. Cleopatra has vigorously resisted Antony's departure; as a soldier he is precisely *not* her servant but makes peace or war as he himself affects. The speech is downright embarrassing; Cleopatra simply pretends not to have heard it: "Cut my lace, Charmian, come—" she says, "But let it be: I am quickly ill, and well, / So Antony loves" (1.3.71–73). Antony's last words to Cleopatra are similarly specious:

> Our separation so abides and flies
> That thou residing here goes yet with me,
> And I hence fleeting here remain with thee.
> Away.
>
> (1.3.102–5)

There is something silly, if not actually dishonest, about this scrap of an Elizabethan valediction poem. It makes a gesture in the direction of ideal love—but so cursory a gesture to so lofty an ideal is a kind of self-contradiction. And apart from its sing-song rhythm, easy rhyme, and conventional ideas, it is quite inappropriate at this moment. For the departure of the man into the man's world of business is an unpleasant inevitability in the lyric poems, whereas everything up to this point has emphasized the element of choice in Antony's departure. The grandeur of "Let Rome in Tiber melt" has been replaced by a feeble convention. In this movement Antony's relations with Cleopatra are only romantic; the flip side of his romanticism is his Roman instinct to limit relations with the Other.

If Antony's language in this first movement reflects the limitations of his relationship to the Other, so, too, do his actions. His marriage to Octavia is doubly significant in this respect. First of all, it is clearly a betrayal of Egypt and Cleopatra. Second, it is also an alliance with a woman who accepts her role as a leisure-time activity and offers no resistance to Antony's life in the world of men. To get things straight from the beginning, Antony intones to his new wife, "The world and my great office will sometimes / Divide me from your bosom" (2.3.1–2). Octavia doesn't skip a beat:

> All the which time
> Before the gods my knee shall bow my prayers
> To them for you.
>
> (2.3.2–4)

Octavia will have no demands to make of her husband that conflict with his demands on himself. Leaving her for good, Antony will later tell her,

> If I lose mine honor,
> I lose myself: better I were not yours
> Than yours so branchless.
>
> (3.4.22–24)

And poor Octavia will not hear the false note. Unlike Cleopatra she is not aware that the appeal to "honor," to his position in the world of men, may mask a breach of faith with her. She sends him off—to Cleopatra, as it turns out—without demur. In choosing Octavia over Cleopatra, Antony tries to choose a *limited* relationship with the Other. Unlike Cleopatra, Octavia offers no threat to the preexisting integrity of the Self.

In the next movement of the play Antony returns to Egypt for good. He does not exactly choose to do so, but his betrayal of Octavia makes another reconciliation with Caesar out of the question. Antony now has nowhere else to go. It is this knowledge that makes the next phase of his relations with Cleopatra so tumultuous and at the same time so much less theatrical than the opening movement of the play. There is no more striking of poses. The first time we see the lovers back together they are not, as we might have expected, dramatizing their reunion; they are holding a strategy session. Of course, it is because of Cleopatra that the strategy they settle on is a disastrous one; they will meet Caesar at sea. Enobarbus is horrified:

> Most worthy sir, you therein throw away
> The absolute soldiership you have by land,
>
> . . . .
>
>   . . . quite forgo
> The way which promises assurance, and
> Give up yourself merely to chance and hazard
> From firm security.
>
>   (3.7.41–42, 45–48)

This is precisely what Antony has done by throwing in his lot with Cleopatra. In his relationship with her he is indeed at sea; he has forgone the assurance of success that Rome promises her sons for the "chance and hazard" of Egypt, Cleopatra, and a life centered on his own sexuality. He is indeed at sea, as all the tragic heroes are when they leave the "firm security" of the patriarchal system and confront the Other dialectically. And at sea Cleopatra is uncontrollable, unfathomable, and possibly unfaithful, even though Antony has committed his worldly fortunes to his relationship with her. Now the antagonism between his worldly affairs and his role as a lover can no longer be glossed over with courtly lies—"thy soldier-servant," etc. Now everything comes out into the open, and the results are those Shakespearean moments when the hero is taken over by sexual loathing:

> I found you as a morsel cold upon
> Dead Caesar's trencher: nay, you were a fragment
> Of Gneius Pompey's, besides what hotter hours,
> Unregist'red in vulgar fame, you have
> Luxuriously picked out. For I am sure,
> Though you can guess what temperance should be,
> You know not what it is.
>
> (3.13.116–22)

The opening of the sexual wound is here, as so often in Shakespeare, a symptom of the hero's confrontation with what Danby calls Nature and what I have been calling the Other. The new world—Egypt and Cleopatra—has become an inevitability for Antony and not merely a pleasure he may choose to enjoy or not. The difficulties of the new world—its ambiguity and its possible hostility to Antony—are now revealed, and Antony responds to the revelation with rage and disbelief. The intensity of his response is now unmistakably genuine; it is no literary convention that prompts his violent "Triple-turned whore!" or his fantasy of Octavia plowing up Cleopatra's face "with her preparèd nails" (4.12.13, 39).

The final phase is one that the heroes never enter until it is too late. In this phase Antony simply abandons judgment of Cleopatra even though he has received no adequate explanation or apology from her. The last phase begins when Cleopatra, who may or may not have betrayed Antony in battle, thinks to avoid his anger by sending him word that she is dead:

> Mardian, go tell him I have slain myself:
> Say that the last I spoke was "Antony"
> And word it, prithee, piteously. Hence, Mardian,
> And bring me how he takes my death.
>
> (4.13.7–10)

The news abruptly turns the tide of Antony's emotions, which had been running heavily against Cleopatra. On hearing it Antony says, "I will o'ertake thee, Cleopatra, and / Weep for my pardon" (4.14.44–45). Cleopatra's supposed suicide is proof to Antony that she has *not* "disposed with Caesar" (4.14.123) and therefore that she has been loyal to himself. Cleopatra becomes "she which by her death our Caesar tells / 'I am conqueror of myself' " (4.14.61–62). When Antony learns that her suicide was a fake, however, his feelings toward her do not undergo another reversal. His anger and hatred do not return. "Bear me," he says immediately on hearing the news, "where Cleopatra bides" (4.14.131); and his last words concern her safety after his death, not the unresolved question of her fidelity to him. In this phase of his story Antony is no longer concerned about Cleopatra as she controls his destiny. It is *her* destiny he thinks of at this point; his own he implicitly trusts to her.

Antony is Shakespeare's most sustained study in the temptation to limit or avoid sexuality where it conflicts with the hero's role in the world of men. The two halves of his life ultimately merge in spite of his efforts to keep them apart: by the second phase of the play Antony's political and personal destinies come together in Egypt. Antony alternately rages against the new world and sadly accepts it; in his dying moments his objections to it seem to have vanished altogether. Antony's final attitude toward Cleopatra is resonant with more than itself. If Cleopatra and Egypt stand for the world we fall into when we discover Nature, then Antony's final unprotesting love for Cleopatra affirms the value of our unsatisfactory natural lives. In his final moments Antony is at peace; he loves what he loves in spite of everything.

Where Danby sees a trend toward exhaustion, disintegration, and "rot[ting] with motion," then, I see a trend toward the recognition and acceptance of the Other. But I cannot claim that the trend I see is very pronounced or that it is powerful enough to counterbalance the disintegrative tendencies of the play. For our glimpse of Antony at peace is very brief. We cannot compare it to our vision of, for instance, Hamlet in *his* final phase. Antony has no graveyard scene, no long still moment when he performs for us his newfound ease. Furthermore, his death does not end the play. What happens to Antony is only part of the story; if we are looking for a sense of resolution we must look at what happens to Cleopatra as well. Does *her* story resolve? Does the fifth act halt the trend toward disintegration, offer an image of something permanent and valuable in human life? If not, then we must agree with Danby that it represents a kind of falling-off from *Hamlet* and *Lear;* Antony's dying words are simply not enough.

Of course, I disagree with Danby. *Antony and Cleopatra,* I think, resolves by offering us an image of a great love relationship. Just as Hamlet and Lear become greatly valuable to us in spite of everything, so too does the relationship between these lovers. This relationship, like whatever is grand about the heroes, endures the confrontation with Nature. It survives the test and resolves the play. But of course we cannot talk about the relationship apart from the lovers who enact it. The confrontation with Nature is endured by both Antony and Cleopatra; having seen something of Antony's relations with Nature we must now turn to Cleopatra's. Cleopatra confronts Nature not as Egypt nor as Antony's Other but as a character with her own destiny at stake.

Does this mean that Cleopatra, alone among Shakespeare's women, is a tragic hero, a version of the Self rather than the Other? Linda Fitz believes that she is. In her revisionist essay "Egyptian Queens and Male Reviewers" ("Egyptian Queens and Male Reviewers: Sexist Attitudes in *Antony and Cleopatra* Criticism," *Shakespeare Quarterly* 28 [1977]), Fitz argues that we must understand Cleopatra from the inside since "Shakespeare . . . takes pains to let Cleopatra explain her contrary behavior and give the reasons for it (1.3)." Cleopatra, according to Fitz, "struggles with her own inconstancy" and "learns and grows as Antony does not." And yet where can we be sure we are getting an inside view of Cleopatra rather than a performance? Only, I think, in act 1, scene 3, the scene Fitz refers to above. This scene is very important to my interpretation as it provides us with an opening through which we can turn the play inside out; through this opening we may see things, as through the wrong end of the opera glasses, from Cleopatra's point of view. But the play does not maintain continuous contact with Cleopatra's point of view; it does not bring us close to Cleopatra for more than a few speeches; it does not give us any insight into the struggles of her inner life. The revelation moment merely tells us of her struggle to keep her lover:

> CHARMIAN. Madam, methinks, if you did love him dearly,
>   You do not hold the method to enforce
>   The like from him.
> CLEOPATRA.   What should I do, I do not?
> CHARMIAN. In each thing give him way, cross him in nothing.
> CLEOPATRA. Thou teachest like a fool: the way to lose him.
>
>   (1.3.6–10)

What we see here is Cleopatra's strategy in dealing with what is outside herself, not any struggle "against her own inconstancy." This exchange does briefly but radically shift the perspective from Antony's to Cleopatra's; and this one shift gives us permission, as it were, to speculate on Cleopatra's motives and goals. It suggests a limited likeness between Cleopatra and the tragic version of Self. But we must acknowledge that our speculative reconstruction of Cleopatra's point of view is a wholly intellectual project. We are not close to Cleopatra, as we are to the tragic hero; we do not sympathize with her or share her hopes and fears. In fact, in the very scenes where the story might evoke most sympathy for her we are most carefully kept at a distance. Whenever Cleopatra suffers loss or defeat she is presented comically, unflatteringly, or ambiguously.

Consider, for instance, the scene in which Cleopatra learns that Antony has married Octavia. Clearly, *she* is *his* victim here and not the other way around. And yet we are dramatically prevented from taking her side, from sympathizing with her against him. She is presented as unreasonable, willful, capricious, and jealous—not as wronged, hurt, or sad. When the messenger arrives she flings herself at him melodramatically until he says in exasperation, "Will't please you hear me?"—to which she characteristically replies, "I have a mind to strike thee ere thou speak'st" (2.5.41–42). The scene proceeds:

CLEOPATRA. Yet, if thou say Antony lives, is well,
  Or friends with Caesar, or not captive to him,
  I'll set thee in a shower of gold, and hail
  Rich pearls upon thee.
MESSENGER.   Madam, he's well.
CLEOPATRA.   Well said.
MESSENGER. And friends with Caesar.
CLEOPATRA.   Th'art an honest man.
MESSENGER. Caesar and he are greater friends than ever.
CLEOPATRA. Make thee a fortune from me.
MESSENGER.   But yet, Madam—
CLEOPATRA. I do not like "But yet"; it does allay
  The good precedence: fie upon "But yet";
  "But yet" is as a jailer to bring forth
  Some monstrous malefactor. Prithee, friend,
  Pour out the pack of matter to mine ear,
  The good and bad together: he's friends with Caesar,
  In state of health, thou say'st, and thou say'st, free.
MESSENGER. Free, madam, no: I made no such report;
  He's bound unto Octavia.
CLEOPATRA.   For what good turn?
MESSENGER. For the best turn i' th' bed.
CLEOPATRA.   I am pale, Charmian.

> MESSENGER. Madam, he's married to Octavia.
> CLEOPATRA. The most infectious pestilence upon thee!
> *Strikes him down.*
>
> (2.5.43–61)

We are elaborately prevented from sharing in Cleopatra's emotions at the very moment when it would be most natural for us to do so.

Another example is the very first skirmish of the play. In the first three scenes Cleopatra struggles to keep her lover from leaving her; by the fourth scene he is gone. And yet the dominant impression left by these scenes is of Cleopatra running circles around Antony, maneuvering him into professions of love only to jeer at them, taunting him with loving Fulvia and with not loving Fulvia, throwing up a fog of accusations and contradictions around Antony's efforts to make a judgment on his situation. Antony, says Danby, is "like the man innocent of jujitsu who thinks he is pushing when really he is being pulled." We may notice, if we like, that at the end of it all the innocent leaves the adept; but we are not free to sympathize very deeply with Cleopatra's loss. We are at least as pleased that Antony has broken away as we are sorry that Cleopatra has been left alone.

But although we do not feel Cleopatra's suffering, we may, if we wish, infer it. We cannot make Emilia the hero of *Othello,* as Carol Neely suggests, nor even Cordelia the hero of *King Lear.* But we can, if we wish, shape a tragic fable around Cleopatra without violating or supplementing the data of the play. Through a glass darkly we can see that she, too, faces the challenge of an unsatisfactory Nature; she, too, resists her diminishment according to its laws. Although at one level she is herself a representative of the Other, she also confronts the Other. The third Cleopatra is in fact the most important one for my interpretation. If we overlook her, the play does not resolve.

Nature (or the Other) in *Antony and Cleopatra,* whether Cleopatra represents it or confronts it, is quite different from Nature in *King Lear.* There Nature consists of starkest good and starkest evil; our difficulty is that the reality of the one may be concealed by the illusion of the other. Here we are faced with no such absolutes. Rather we are faced with an acceptable level of niggling everyday selfishness, with the perfectly understandable compromises we make, with ordinary failures of clarity and courage. Loss and defeat are undramatic here; no one stands on the heath and roars with astonishment and pain. In most of Shakespeare's tragedies, as A. C. Bradley notes [in his *Oxford Lectures on Poetry*], we are confronted early on with "scenes of action or passion which agitate the audience with alarm, horror, painful expectation, or absorbing sympathies and antipathies." What is there of this in the first three acts of *Antony and Cleopatra*? "Almost nothing. People converse, discuss, accuse one another, excuse themselves, mock, describe, drink together, arrange a marriage, meet and part; but they do not kill, do not even tremble or weep." In *Antony and Cleopatra* the thing in nature that works against the characters is undramatic and diffuse; nevertheless it grinds away. In almost every scene some character is shown by his own or another's analysis to be smaller than he would like to think himself. Ventidius tells us that Antony is not free from jealousy of his own lieutenants (3.1); Antony tells us that the loyalties of the common people are shifty and perverse (1.3); Pompey tells Menas that his own honor depends on technicalities (2.7); Charmian reminds Cleopatra that she has loved before (1.4); Antony notices his own inconstancy toward Fulvia:

> What our contempts doth often hurl from us,
> We wish it ours again. The present pleasure,
> By revolution low'ring, does become
> The opposite of itself: she's good, being gone;
> The hand could pluck her back that shoved her on.
>
> (1.2.124–28)

All of these speeches imply that there are no absolutes, no unambiguous goods—or that even if there are, human nature can never adhere to them long enough to matter.

Such is the Nature that Shakespeare deals with in *Antony and Cleopatra*, Danby to the contrary. And just as Lear's accomplishment is appropriate to the Nature of that play, so Antony's and Cleopatra's are appropriate to this. In *King Lear*, where warring cosmological forces seem in danger of overwhelming the significance of the human drama, Lear's search for value and joy takes on a kind of religious intensity. In *Antony and Cleopatra* it is much harder to know where to have the enemy, for here we are dealing not with the inhuman but with the all-too-human. If Lear's achievement is the depths to which he can root himself in such unfriendly soil, Antony-and-Cleopatra's perhaps, is in rising above the undergrowth of everyday failure into the sunshine of history, myth, story. Antony and Cleopatra do become famous, historical. Their ambition is to make themselves special, and as we shall see, they do.

Antony and Cleopatra, of course, do not struggle as a couple against Nature; they struggle individually, and they often appear to be struggling against each other. For if Cleopatra often represents Nature to Antony, often he represents it to her. But although at one level there is conflict between them, their separate and individual campaigns against Nature are at another level complementary. There is a third and final dialectic in the opposition between their different modes of meeting the challenge of Nature; it is the resolution to this dialectic that resolves the play.

Antony struggles with Nature by struggling with himself; Cleopatra has no quarrel with herself and struggles exclusively with the outside world. Whereas Antony resists his decline by struggling to become his own ideal, Cleopatra struggles only to keep her lover, to outfox Caesar, to win admiration from all. She is aware of no gap between what she is and what she ought to be, only of the gap between what she wants and what she has. Even when we put Cleopatra in the position of the striving Self, we must notice that she struggles as an Other, as a fixed identity. She is not self-divided, like the tragic heroes; she is at work on her destiny but not, like them, on herself.

Antony struggles to control his destiny by taking control of himself. "Ten thousand harms," he tells himself in act 1, scene 2, "my idleness doth hatch," and so he resolves to be less idle. He decides to become a good Roman again and urges the messenger

> Speak to me home, mince not the general tongue:
> Name Cleopatra as she is called in Rome;
> Rail thou in Fulvia's phrase, and taunt my faults
> With such full license as both truth and malice
> Have power to utter.
>
> (1.2.106–10)

Antony wants to hear his "ills" so he can mend them. He fights his sense of dissolving identity—of submission to the play's occasions—with the weapons of self-consciousness and willpower. Although the decisions he takes about his character are often impossible to carry out, he is always sincere in his resolutions. It is the essence of the battle he wages against Nature that he should always believe he means what he says. He tells Octavia, "I have not kept my square, but that to come / Shall all be done by th' rule" (2.3.6–7), and he means it, even though thirty lines later he decides to return to Cleopatra. When he fails to live up to his resolutions he is bitter in his self-recriminations: "I have fled myself, and have instructed cowards / To run and show their shoulders" (3.11.7–8). He is always ready to accept instruction; when Cleopatra, in the first words we see her address to him since he left for Rome, advises him that "Celerity is never more admired / Than by the negligent," he answers,

> A good rebuke,
> Which might have well becomed the best of men
> To taunt at slackness.
>
> (3.7.24–27)

Finally, when he thinks that Cleopatra has killed herself and sees Eros do so, he takes their deeds as a lesson:

> Thrice-nobler than myself,
> Thou teachest me, O valiant Eros, what
> I should, and thou couldst not. My queen and Eros
> Have by their brave instruction got upon me
> A nobleness in record.
>
> (4.14.95–99)

All these are efforts to be the man he thinks he should be; Antony is always at work on himself. Cleopatra, on the other hand, reproaches herself with nothing, rejects her past when it does not do her honor ("My salad days"—[1.5.73]), makes no resolutions for the future, and takes instruction from no one. She is fighting Nature with quite different weapons. If Antony tries to be a center that will hold, Cleopatra seems anxious to appear the least coherent thing on the landscape. Antony aims for constancy, of identity and of Fortune; Cleopatra reveals the constancy of her identity through her extravagant feigning and controls her Fortune by changing roles faster than it requires her to do. Instead of aiming for a solidity of personality that will control her universe, she risks everything on her capacity to fly faster than the Fortune that pursues her.

The crucial speech by which to distinguish between the two modes is Antony's great meditation on his own sense of shapelessness:

> Sometimes we see a cloud that's dragonish,
> A vapor sometime like a bear or lion,
> A tower citadel, a pendant rock,
> A forkèd mountain, or blue promontory
> With trees upon't that nod unto the world

And mock our eyes with air.

. . . .

My good knave Eros, now thy captain is
Even such a body: here I am Antony,
Yet cannot hold this visible shape, my knave.

(4.14.2–7, 12–14)

Antony here is divided from himself, disappointed in himself and uncertain of his own identity. Cleopatra has no such speech; it is of the essence of Cleopatra, even of this third, possibly suffering Cleopatra, that she should have no such speech. Even as she passes through the phases of the tragic fable Cleopatra never comments on herself with disapproval, never shares with us the slightest dissatisfaction in herself. Her commentary is always (at least in part) a performance. Since we are aware of no seams in her personality, since there are no openings through which we can have at her innermost soul, she appears to us, as she does to Antony, mysterious and perfect-unto-herself. Antony's description of Egypt's emblematic animal, the crocodile, applies quite as well to Egypt's queen:

It is shaped, sir, like itself, and it is as broad as it hath breadth; it is just so high as it is, and moves with its own organs.

(2.7.43–45)

Whereas Antony anatomizes himself for us, telling us his shape and breadth and height at each point in the play, Cleopatra never does. So though we seem to see as clearly as Antony the varying shapes he assumes, we can only say that Cleopatra, like the crocodile, is as broad as she has breadth.

The difference between Antony's and Cleopatra's styles of confronting Nature may be illustrated by a comparison between his dealings with Caesar and hers. Both are underdogs when they first face him; other than that the scenes that they stage have nothing in common. Before the meeting between Caesar and Antony early in act 2, Enobarbus suggests that Antony may lose his temper. "If Caesar move him," says Enobarbus, "Let Antony look over Caesar's head / And speak as loud as Mars" (2.2.4–6). But of course Antony does no such thing. His final speech of the argument is as follows:

As nearly as I may,
I'll play the penitent to you: but mine honesty

Shall not make poor my greatness, nor my power
Work without it. Truth is, that Fulvia,
To have me out of Egypt, made wars here,
For which myself, the ignorant motive, do
So far ask pardon as befits mine honor
To stoop in such a case.

(2.2.91–98)

Antony, as usual, is trying to bind together expediency, or responsibility, to the Idea of Antony. He uses his authentic self in the battle for his destiny; his dignity and fair-mindedness rather than his excuses are the answers that he makes to Caesar's accusations. It is a very impressive and admirable speech; there is poise and confidence in the way that Antony walks the line between chest-thumping and self-deprecation. Yet, Nature being what it is in the play, the truth that Antony achieves by confronting destiny this way is vulnerable to an immediate and unanswerable attack:

ENOBARBUS. Or, if you borrow one another's love for the
    instant, you may, when you hear no more words of
    Pompey, return it again: you shall have time to wran-
    gle in when you have nothing else to do.
ANTONY. Thou art a soldier only; speak no more.
ENOBARBUS. That truth should be silent I had almost forgot.
ANTONY. You wrong this presence; therefore speak no more.
ENOBARBUS. Go to, then; your considerate stone.

(2.2.103–11)

Because Antony opts for a version of sincerity, his compromises with expediency leave him vulnerable to cynicism.

Cleopatra, on the other hand, never bothers to put the pieces of herself in truthful relation to one another and is therefore not vulnerable to an attack on the final assembly. She leaves the pieces of her identity false, because fragmentary, and flings them at the agents of her declining Fortunes. When she finds herself at a disadvantage before Caesar, she plays her part with an extravagance that would be unthinkable in Antony. Toward the end of the play, "I'll take my leave," says Caesar to Cleopatra after a few polite threats. Cleopatra dramatically and unnecessarily answers him,

And may, through all the world: 'tis yours, and we,
Your scutcheons and your signs of conquest, shall

> Hang in what place you please.
> (5.2.133–36)

The difference between Antony's balanced apology and Cleopatra's abandoned self-abnegation is not due to the deterioration of the political situation between the one and the other. It is due to the fact that Antony always plays himself as nearly as he can, whereas Cleopatra purposely keeps herself separate from her roles.

Antony takes the straight path to sincerity and finds it mined by his own slightly tainted motives. Cleopatra's brand of sincerity brings to mind a passage in Mailer's *Advertisements for Myself* in which Mailer comments on his own search for an authentic style: "To write about myself is to send my style through a circus of variations and postures, a fireworks of virtuosity designed to achieve . . . I do not even know what. Leave it that I become a quick-change artist, as if I believe I can trap the Prince of Truth in the act of switching a style." But although Cleopatra is also a quick-change artist, Mailer's passage is actually a better description of Hamlet than of Cleopatra. Hamlet's variations and postures are designed to achieve . . . he does not know what. Cleopatra's are purposive rather than exploratory. They are not cultures to nourish the embryo of her final, fully developed being; they are deployed by a preexisting identity on missions in its own interests. Like the women in the comedies, and unlike Hamlet, Cleopatra is revealed and not changed by her actions. In a play that is crisscrossed by journeys all over the Mediterranean, Cleopatra alone stays at home. She is no quester; she makes no odyssey in search of herself.

The relevant comparison here is with Octavia, who journeys from Rome to Athens and back again in the effort to reconcile the two men by whom she is defined. It would seem, in act 5, that Cleopatra is caught between these same two men, for it has been made clear through the imagery that an alliance with Caesar would be a sexual matter and amount to a betrayal of Antony. Caesar's metaphor, as he looks forward to his conquest of her, is of sexual capitulation:

> Women are not
> In their best fortunes strong, but want will perjure
> The ne'er-touched vestal.
> (3.12.29–31)

But Cleopatra, unlike Octavia, defines herself. Her changes of style are not experiments in a new identity as Caesar's ally but rather attempts to flush out the danger to her soul that she senses in Caesar. She is faced not with a choice between men but with a threat to her own identity. It is through her fidelity to herself that she is ultimately faithful to Antony, although it is no coincidence that this should be true. Antony recognizes her, Caesar would ruin her. Octavia, having no identity of her own, cannot be said to have been faithful to either man. *Her* fidelity simply doesn't matter, whereas Cleopatra's does.

And this, in fact, has been Cleopatra's goal all along—to make herself matter. Antony struggles with the problem of judgment, thinking that to make his mark on the world he must make correct distinctions between right and wrong, true and false, Rome and Egypt, honor and love. Cleopatra does not bother to make judgments. She meets her occasions with whatever she can find within herself, authentic or not, that will give her the edge. Just as she tries to make herself interesting rather than pleasing to Antony, so she tries always to be the one who elicits judgments rather than the one who makes them. She has no use for Charmian's advice, "In time we hate that which we often fear" (1.3.12). It does not matter whether Antony's emotions toward her are good or bad; what matters is that he should not be able to leave off trying to figure her out.

At his death scene Antony gives Cleopatra a nugget of absolute, Roman advice: trust Proculeius. But like all his efforts to make absolute judgments, this one is a failure. Proculeius betrays and captures her. So Cleopatra once again switches styles. When Dolabella appears, he asks her to say that she has heard of him, but she refuses to make even such a trivial judgment of him as this. Instead, she forces him to judge her. At the end of her speech "I dreamt there was an Emperor Antony" (5.2.76 et seq.), she asks him, "Think you there was or might be such a man / As this I dreamt of?" (5.2.93–94), and Dolabella answers, "Gentle madam, no." But it does not matter that his judgment is negative; for what is at issue is not her truth, but the validity of her claim to be the center of attention, the topic of conversation, the object of judgment. And Dolabella, although he rejects her version of Antony, accepts her greatness:

> Your loss is as yourself, great; and you bear it
> As answering to the weight. Would I might never
> O'ertake pursued success, but I do feel,
> By the rebound of yours, a grief that smites
> My very heart at root.
>
> (5.2.101–5)

Seeing that her work is done, Cleopatra does not waste any further time: "I thank you, sir. / Know you what Caesar means to do with me?" (5.2.105–6). And of course Dolabella tells her what she needs to know: that Caesar means to lead her in triumph through the streets of Rome. Now she knows how to behave.

Because Antony tries to define himself within Nature, his moments of authenticity, although they compel our sympathy and admiration, must be transient and qualified. Even the noble love in the scene where he thanks his followers is subject to a moment of irony: "What does he mean?" asks Cleopatra, and Enobarbus replies, "To make his followers weep" (4.2.23–24). Cleopatra, however, does not try to enact her "true self." She means to break through the limit on human stature—on the "true self" that is imposed by this play's Nature. To do so, she must abandon conventional standards of truth and decency, and she does so without regrets. So whereas we see in Antony a moving and admirable achievement given the restrictions of Nature and of his own human nature, Cleopatra presents us with a double vision of what lies outside the normal human limits. Her kind of truth is absolute and permanent, but it must coexist with patent lies. For instance, Mardian, sent to tell Antony that Cleopatra has killed herself, says, "My mistress loved thee, and her fortunes mingled / With thine entirely" (4.14.24–25). This is simultaneously a disgraceful lie and the simple truth. In context it is monstrously untrue; in retrospect it describes the story. Or Enobarbus, anticipating hysterics when Antony announces his departure, says,

> Cleopatra, catching but the least noise of this, dies instantly;
> I have seen her die twenty times upon far poorer moment. I
> do think there is mettle in death, which commits some loving
> act upon her, she hath such a celerity in dying.
>
> (1.2.141–45)

This hits its mark at the time and yet it all comes true. For although celerity is a Roman virtue and Caesar's weapon in the power struggle with Antony and Pompey, Cleopatra is too quick for him. He "hath sent— / Too slow a messenger" (5.2.321). "The stroke of death" *is* at the end "as a lover's pinch" (5.2.295), and Antony's final departure *does* make Cleopatra's death inevitable. Again and again we find ourselves having to say of Cleopatra's lies, "And that's *true*, too."

These, then, are the two modes of confronting Nature in this play: the one humanistic, synthesizing, responsible; the other self-assertive, divisive, flamboyant, amoral. Antony is, or tries to be, sincere; he struggles to know himself and to act in accordance with his knowledge. Conversely, when his actions betray his sense of Self he struggles to change. Cleopatra has no part in the effort to accommodate action and inner life. She is not, like the tragic hero, a divided self, struggling to pull herself together. Her struggle is only to discover and ward off what threatens her, to do battle with the outside world, not with the one within. Like all Shakespeare's women, she is a finished product, a preexisting unified identity. We become aware of Cleopatra's inner life only insofar as it serves her conscious purposes; it is not, like Antony's, subversive, demanding, beyond his control.

Linda Fitz argues that Cleopatra's inner life *is* subversive of her conscious purposes and that there is drama in her struggle to take control of it. The triumphant outcome of her struggle, according to Fitz, comes when Cleopatra says,

> My resolution's placed, and I have nothing
> Of woman in me; now from head to foot
> I am marble-constant: now the fleeting moon
> No planet is of mine.
>
> (5.2.238–41)

And just as this speech indicates the successful conclusion of her struggle against her own inconstancy, so the following speech represents the culmination of the spiritual growth we expect in a tragic hero:

> No more but e'en a woman, and commanded
> By such poor passion as the maid that milks
> And does the meanest chares.
>
> (4.15.76–78)

It is worth noticing, however, that these two speeches contradict one another. Marble-constancy is incompatible with milkmaid passion. To be commanded by passion is not to command oneself, as Cleopatra claims to do. These two speeches are best understood, I think, as performances which *use* the inner life rather than as direct expressions of it. What is moving is neither Cleopatra's marble-constancy nor her new simplicity, but the sheer energy, talent, and effort she puts into her performances.

Cleopatra herself comments on the energy it takes to perform as she does. The comment comes after the one moment in which she abandons or fails at performance; when Antony is leaving her in act 1 she is at a loss for words:

> Courteous lord, one word.
> Sir, you and I must part, but that's not it:
> Sir, you and I have loved, but there's not it:
> That you know well. Something it is I would—
> O, my oblivion is a very Antony,
> And I am all forgotten.
>
> (1.3.86–91)

The broken sentences create the effect of an emotion beyond even Cleopatra's prodigious capacities to perform; in contrast to Antony's glibly rhetorical farewell speeches, Cleopatra's farewell is a demonstration of speechlessness. Antony, with Othello-like obtuseness, responds to this one display of naked emotion with disapproval:

> But that your royalty
> Holds idleness your subject, I should take you
> For idleness itself.
>
> (1.3.91–93)

Cleopatra responds,

> 'Tis sweating labor
> To bear such idleness so near the heart
> As Cleopatra this.
>
> (1.3.93–95)

Cleopatra, unlike Antony, does not deny that she performs her love, plays roles, puts on shows. She only claims that it is hard work, "sweating labor," to put on these particular shows, and that it is hard because the performance concerns something "so near the heart." She only says so this once; but we would do well, I think, to remember this speech when we come to act 5, where the project near her heart is the preservation of her own integrity. If we are too aware of the sweating labor, of course, we lose the effect of the performance—just as we lose the effect when we become aware of the actual sweat on a ballerina. But if we are unaware of the effort and risk of her performance altogether, then it must seem to us, as it seems to Antony, idle. Like our appreciation of live ballet, our appreciation of Cleopatra's act depends on our understanding of how hard it is to do it.

In *The Dickens Theatre*, Robert Garis identifies two schools of performance, one of which he associates with Duse and the other with Bernhardt. Duse, he says, offers the continuous illusion of realism, whereas Bernhardt is overtly theatrical. Garis quotes Shaw on Bernhardt to illustrate his point:

> One is not sorry to have been coaxed to relax one's notions of the dignity of art when she gets to serious business and shows how ably she does her work. The coaxing suits well with the childishly egotistical character of her acting, which is not the art of making you think more highly or feel more deeply, but the art of making you admire her, pity her, champion her, weep with her, laugh at her jokes, follow her fortunes breathlessly, and applaud her wildly when the curtain falls. It is the art of finding out all your weaknesses and practising on them—cajoling you, harrowing you, exciting you—on the whole, fooling you. And it is always Sarah Bernhardt in her own capacity who does this to you. The dress, the title of the play, the order of the words may vary; but the woman is always the same. She does not enter into the leading character: she substitutes herself for it.

If Cleopatra's role is the enactment of her inner life, Shaw's description of Bernhardt may illuminate her method. Whereas Antony tries to enact his feelings as accurately as he can, Cleopatra, à la Bernhardt, seems to substitute herself for her feelings. "Here I am Cleopatra"—is the message of the "marble-constant" speech—"feeling the thrill of my own resolution." And in the milkmaid speech: "Here I am Cleopatra feeling the bittersweet pleasure of illusionlessness." I do not mean that Cleopatra is pretending to feel something she does not; I only mean that her feelings do not threaten her consciousness of being herself, Cleopatra, as broad as she has breadth, at all times and places. Under similar circumstances of loss, the tragic Self, by contrast, invariably suffers a loss of identity more painful than the material loss itself.

Cleopatra's style of confronting Nature is, of course, a function of her gender. Only the feminine Other faces the challenge of Nature, of the world outside the Self, with an identity as fixed and unyielding as Nature itself. Insofar as she does confront this challenge, Cleopatra is a rarity among Shakespeare's women characters and has some affinity with the masculine tragic Self. But insofar as she faces it with performances à la Bernhardt, insofar as her performances remain perfectly self-centered and in her own control, she remains Other even in the face of the Other, in the face of Nature and the challenge of tragedy. Although she is certainly the coprotagonist of the play, she is not the representative of the Self; she is not, as Linda Fitz suggests, a tragic hero.

It is time to return to the question raised by Danby's essay, the question of tragic climax or resolution. Neither Antony nor Cleopatra as individuals provides us with a resolution, with an image of human value so impressive as to triumph over and transform our sense of Nature. But what is between them, their relationship, does endure, does restore them to history. The forward motion of the play destroys them both as individuals; nevertheless, it "proves" the relationship between them. This relationship is complex; they are both married and not married. They are not married in that each would sacrifice the other, if they could, for the sake of their own separate destinies; they are married in that they cannot. Antony follows Cleopatra out of the sea battle against his will because "My heart was to thy rudder tied by th' strings" (3.11.57), and Cleopatra remains faithful to Antony because, although she could wish it were otherwise, it is the only way of being "noble to myself" (5.2.191). But out of the antagonism between their immediate purposes comes the accomplishment of their ultimate purpose, the achievement of distinction or historicity. They defeat themselves in the short run; Cleopatra destroys Antony in her attempt to possess him, and Antony cannot deny her even when he knows she is doing so. Yet they succeed in becoming famous, not individually, but as a pair. In trying to serve themselves, they have served the third thing, their story, and thus have served each other as well as themselves.

If Antony had not resisted Cleopatra's spell, he would have lost his citizenship in the world of men, and Cleopatra would not have had an Emperor Antony to dream of when she needed one. But if Antony had succeeded in breaking away, if, Othello-like, he had taken decisive action against the treacherous witch, there would have been no Cleopatra to make a myth of Antony and to pay him the returns on his love that she finally does. In other words, Antony controls his fortune by allowing its agent, Cleopatra, to destroy him, for it is only after his death that she is in a position to choose Antony without qualification. Had he not realized this, Antony's fate would have been that of a strumpet's fool; but because he cannot help giving her her due, she lives to make her choice and to give him a noble fate. Her death for his sake is ambiguous, for it is primarily a self-protective measure; his death for her sake is equally ambiguous, for he fights it every step of the way. Yet in this play, it is the negative way to love that leads to significance, to a place in the story. The Octavias and Lepiduses get lost precisely because they lack images of themselves that would command their first loyalty, whereas Antony and Cleopatra are each ennobled by the other's love only because each pursues a private destiny. Danby remarks that in *Antony and Cleopatra* "Opposites are juxtaposed, mingled, married; then from the very union which seems to promise strength, dissolution flows." Yet if we see Cleopatra as opposite to Antony, we see that here is one pair of contrarieties that do *not* mingle, and the fame that each earns from his connection with the other depends on the space between them.

The third Cleopatra, then, is the one we must turn to in order to account for our sense of resolution at the end of the play. This Cleopatra faces Nature independently of Antony and differently from him; ultimately, it is her own self-centeredness that leads her back to him. He, by contrast, repeatedly returns to Cleopatra by *decentering*, by abandoning his pride, his sense of his due, the images he has of himself. This double movement of each, in their opposite ways, toward the other provides us with the resolution we have come to expect in Shakespearean tragedy. As in *King Lear*, the third thing is love.

Virtus under Erasure

Jonathan Dollimore

In Jonson's *Sejanus*, Silius, about to take his own life in order to escape the persecution of Tiberius, tells the latter: "The means that makes your greatness, must not come / In mention of it" (3.311–12). He is of course exposing a strategy of power familiar to the period: first there occurs an effacement of the material conditions of its possibility, second, a claim for its transcendent origin, one ostensibly legitimating it and putting it beyond question—hence Tiberius's invocation only moments before of "the Capitol, / . . . all our Gods . . . the dear Republic, / Our sacred Laws, and just authority" (3.216–18). In *Sejanus* this is transparent enough. In other plays—I choose for analysis here *Antony and Cleopatra* and *Coriolanus*—the representation of power is more complex in that we are shown how the ideology in question constitutes not only the authority of those in power but their very identity.

Staged in a period in which there occurred the unprecedented decline of the power, military and political, of the titular aristocracy, *Antony* and *Coriolanus*, like *Sejanus* before them, substantiate the contention that "'tis place, / Not blood, discerns the noble, and the base" (*Sejanus*, 5.1.11–12). Historical shifts in power together with the recognition, or at least a more public acknowledgement of, its actual operations, lead to the erasure of older notions of honour and *virtus*. Both plays effect a sceptical interrogation of martial ideology and in

From *Radical Tragedy: Religion, Ideology, and Power in the Drama of Shakespeare and His Contemporaries.* © 1984 by Jonathan Dollimore. Harvester, 1984.

doing so foreground the complex social and political relations which hitherto it tended to occlude.

In his study of English drama in the seventeenth century C. L. Barber detects a significant decline in the presence of honour as a martial ideal and he is surely right to interpret this as due to changes in the nature and occupations of the aristocracy during that period. These included the professionalising of warfare and the increasing efficiency of state armies. The effect of such changes was that by the end of the seventeenth century there was considerably less scope for personal military initiative and military glory; honour becomes an informal personal code with an extremely attenuated social dimension (*The Idea of Honour in the English Drama 1591–1700*).

More recently, and even more significantly for the present study, Mervyn James has explored in depth the changing conceptions of honour between 1485 and 1642; most striking is his conclusion that there occurred "a change of emphasis, apparent by the early seventeenth century . . . [involving] . . . the emergence of a 'civil' society in which the monopoly both of honour and violence by the state was asserted" (*English Politics and the Concept of Honour 1485–1642*).

Such are the changes which activate a contradiction latent in martial ideology and embodied in two of Shakespeare's protagonists, Antony and Coriolanus. From one perspective—becoming but not yet residual—they appear innately superior and essentially autonomous, their power independent of the political context in which it finds expression. In short they possess that *virtus* which enables each, in Coriolanus's words, to "stand / As if a man were author of himself" (5.3.35–36). "As if": even as these plays reveal the ideological scope of that belief they disclose the alternative emergent perspective, one according to which Antony and Coriolanus are nothing more than their reputation, an ideological effect of powers antecedent to and independent of them. Even as each experiences himself as the origin and embodiment of power, he is revealed in the words of Foucault to be its instrument and effect—its instrument because, first and foremost, its effect. Bacon brilliantly focusses this contradiction in his essay on martial glory: "It was prettily devised of Æsop: *The fly sate upon the axle-tree of the chariot wheel, and said, What a dust do I raise!*" (*Essays*). Throughout Bacon's essay there is a dryly severe insistence on that fact which martial ideology cannot internally accommodate: "opinion brings on substance." Such is the condition of Antony and Coriolanus, and increasingly so: as they transgress the power structure which constitutes them both their political and personal identities—inextricably bound together if not identical—disintegrate.

VIRTUS AND HISTORY

Antony and Cleopatra anticipates the dawn of a new age of imperialist consolidation:

> The time of universal peace is near.
> Prove this a prosp'rous day, the three nook'd world
> Shall bear the olive freely.
>
> (4.6.5–7)

Prior to such moments heroic *virtus* may appear to be identical with the dominant material forces and relations of power. But this is never actually so: they were only ever coterminous and there is always the risk that a new historical conjuncture will throw them into misalignment. This is what happens in *Antony and Cleopatra*; Antony, originally identified in terms of both *virtus* and these dominant forces and relations, is destroyed by their emerging disjunction.

In an important book Eugene Waith has argued that "Antony's reassertion of his heroic self in the latter part of the play is entirely personal. What he reasserts is individual integrity. . . . Heroism rather than heroic achievement becomes the important thing" (*The Herculean Hero*). On this view Antony privately reconstitutes his "heroic self" despite or maybe even because of being defeated by circumstances beyond his control. I want to argue that the reverse is true: heroism of Antony's kind can never be "entirely personal" (as indeed Bacon insisted) nor separated from either "heroic achievement" or the forces and relations of power which confer its meaning.

The reader persuaded by the Romantic reading of this play is likely to insist that I'm missing the point—that what I've proposed is at best only true of the world in which Antony and Cleopatra live, a world transcended by their love, a love which "translineates man (sic) to divine likeness" (Wilson Knight, *The Imperial Theme*). It is not anti-Romantic moralism which leads me to see this view as wholly untenable. In fact I want to argue for an interpretation of the play which refuses the usual critical divide whereby it is either "a tragedy of lyrical inspiration, justifying love by presenting it as triumphant over death, or . . . a remorseless exposure of human frailties, a presentation of spiritual possibilities dissipated through a senseless surrender to passion" (Traversi, *An Approach to Shakespeare*). Nor do I discount the Romantic reading by wilfully disregarding the play's captivating poetry: it is, indeed, on occasions rapturously expressive of desire. But the language of desire, far from transcending the power relations which structure this society, is wholly in-formed by them.

As a preliminary instance of this, consider the nature of Antony's belated "desire" for Fulvia, expressed at news of her death and not so dissimilar to his ambivalent desire for Cleopatra (as the sudden shift of attention from the one to the other suggests):

> Thus did I desire it:
> What our contempts doth often hurl from us
> We wish it ours again; the present pleasure,
> By revolution low'ring, does become
> The opposite of itself. She's good, being gone;
> The hand could pluck her back that shov'd her on.
> I must from this enchanting queen break off.
>
> (1.2.119–25)

True, the language of the final scenes is very different from this, but there too we are never allowed to forget that the moments of sublimity are conditional upon absence, nostalgic contemplation upon the fact that the other is irrevocably gone. As for present love, it is never any the less conditioned by the imperatives of power than the arranged marriage between Antony and Octavia.

VIRTUS AND REALPOLITIK

In *Antony and Cleopatra* those with power make history yet only in accord with the contingencies of the existing historical moment—in Antony's words: "the strong necessity of time" (1.3.42). If this sounds fatalistic, in context it is quite clear that Antony is not capitulating to "Time" as such but engaging in *realpolitik*, real power relations. His capacity for policy is in fact considerable; not only, and most obviously, is there the arranged marriage with Octavia, but also those remarks of his which conclude the alliance with Lepidus and Caesar against Pompey:

> [Pompey] hath laid strange courtesies and great
> Of late upon me. I must thank him only,
> Lest my remembrance suffer ill report;
> At heel of that, defy him.
>
> (2.2.159–62)

In fact, the suggestion of fatalism in Antony's reference to time is itself strategic, an evasive displacing of responsibility for his impending departure from Cleopatra. As such it is parallelled later by Caesar when he tells the distraught Octavia,

> Be you not troubled with the time, which drives
> O'er your content these strong necessities,
> But let determin'd things to destiny
> Hold unbewail'd their way.

> (3.6.82–85)

The cause of her distress is divided allegiance between brother and husband (Caesar and Antony) who are now warring with each other. Caesar's response comes especially ill from one scarcely less responsible for her conflict than Antony; her marriage to the latter was after all dictated by his political will: "The *power* of Caesar, and / His *power* unto Octavia" (2.2.147–48, my italics). "Time" and "destiny" mystify power by eclipsing its operation and effect, and Caesar knows this; compare the exchange on Pompey's galley—ANTONY: "Be a child o' th' time. / CAESAR: Possess it, I'll make answer" (2.7.98–99). Caesar, in this respect, is reminiscent of Machiavelli's Prince; he is inscrutable and possessed of an identity which becomes less fixed, less identifiable as his power increases. Antony by contrast is defined in terms of omnipotence (the more so, paradoxically, as his power diminishes): the "man of men" (1.4.72), the "lord of lords" (4.8.16).

In both *Antony and Cleopatra* and *Coriolanus* the sense of *virtus* (virtue) is close to "valour," as in "valour is the chiefest virtue" (*Coriolanus*, 2.2.82), but with the additional and crucial connotations of self-sufficiency and autonomous power, as in "Trust to thy *single virtue*; for thy soldiers / . . . have . . . / Took their discharge" (*King Lear*, 5.3.104–6). The essentialist connotations of "virtue" are also clearly brought out in a passage from *Troilus and Cressida* discussed [elsewhere]: "what hath mass or matter by itself / Lies rich in virtue and unmingled." In *Antony and Cleopatra* this idea of self-sufficiency is intensified to such an extent that it suggests a transcendent autonomy; thus Cleopatra calls Antony "lord of lords! / O *infinite virtue*, com'st thou smiling from / The world's great snare uncaught?" (4.8.16–18). Coriolanus is similarly described as proud, "even to the altitude of his virtue" (2.1.38). Against this is a counter-discourse, one denying that virtue is the source and ethical legitimation of power and suggesting instead that the reverse is true—in the words of Macro in *Sejanus*, "A prince's power makes all his actions virtue" (3.717). At the beginning of act 3 for example Silius urges Ventidius further to consolidate his recent successes in war, so winning even greater gratitude from Antony. Ventidius replies that, although "Caesar and Antony have ever won / More in their officer than person" (3.1.16–17), an officer of theirs who makes that fact too apparent will lose, not gain favour. It is an exchange which nicely illustrates the way power is a function not of the "person" (l. 17) but of "place" (l. 12), and that the criterion for reward is not intrinsic to the "performance" (l. 27) but, again, relative to one's placing in the power structure (cf. *Sejanus*, 3.302–5: "all best turns / With doubtful princes, turn deep injuries / In estimation, when they greater rise, / Than can be answered").

Later in the same act Antony challenges Caesar to single combat (3.13.20–28). It is an attempt to dissociate Caesar's power from his individual virtue. Enobarbus, amazed at the stupidity of this, testifies to the reality Antony is trying, increasingly, to deny:

> men's judgements are
> A parcel of their fortunes, and things outward
> Do draw the inward quality after them,
> To suffer all alike.
>
> (3.13.31–34)

In Enobarbus's eyes, Antony's attempt to affirm a self-sufficient identity confirms *exactly the opposite*. Correspondingly, Caesar scorns Antony's challenge with a simple but devastating repudiation of its essentialist premise: because "twenty times of better fortune" than Antony, he is, correspondingly, "twenty men to one" (4.2.3–4).

As effective power slips from Antony he becomes obsessed with reasserting his sense of himself as (in his dying words): "the greatest prince o' th' world, / The noblest" (4.20.54–55). The contradiction inherent in this is clear; it is indeed as Canidius remarks: "his whole action grows / Not in the power on't" (3.7.68–69). Antony's conception of his omnipotence narrows in proportion to the obsessiveness of his wish to reassert it; eventually it centres on the sexual anxiety—an assertion of sexual prowess—which has characterised his relationship with both Cleopatra and Caesar from the outset. He several times dwells on the youthfulness of Caesar in comparison with his own age (e.g., at 3.13.20, 4.12.48) and is generally preoccupied with lost youthfulness (e.g., at 3.13.192; 4.4.26; 4.8.22). During the battle scenes of acts 3 and 4 he keeps reminding Cleopatra of his prowess—militaristic and sexual: "I will appear in blood" (2.13.174); "There's sap in't yet! The next time I do fight, / I'll make death love me" (3.13.192–93); and:

> leap thou, attire and all,
> Through proof of harness to my heart, and there
> Ride on the pants triumphing.
>
> (4.8.14–16)

All this, including the challenge to single combat with Caesar, becomes an obsessive attempt on the part of an ageing warrior (the "old ruffian"—[4.1.4]) to reassert his virility, not only to Cleopatra but also to Caesar, his principal male competitor. Correspondingly, his willingness to risk everything by fighting on Caesar's terms (3.7) has much more to do with reckless overcompensation for his own experienced powerlessness, his fear of impotence, than the largesse of a noble soul. His increasing ambivalence towards Cleopatra further bespeaks that insecurity (e.g., at 3.12 and 4.12). When servants refuse to obey him he remarks "Authority melts from me"—but insists nevertheless "I am / Antony yet" (3.13.92–93): even as he is attempting to deny it Antony is acknowledging that identity is crucially dependent upon power. Moments later even he cannot help remarking the difference between "what I am" and "what . . . I was" (3.13.142–43).

It is only when the last vestiges of his power are gone that the myth of heroic omnipotence exhausts itself, even for him. In place of his essentialist fixedness, "the firm Roman," the "man of steel" he once felt himself to be (1.4.43; 4.4.35), Antony now experiences himself in extreme dissolution:

> That which is now a horse, even with a thought
> The rack dislimns, and makes it indistinct
> As water is in water . . .
> Eros, now thy captain is
> Even such a body: here I am Antony,
> Yet cannot hold this visible shape
>
> (4.4.9–14)

Virtus, divorced from the power structure, has left to it only the assertion of a negative, inverted autonomy: "there is left us / Ourselves to end ourselves" (4.14.21–22). And in an image which effectively expresses the contradiction Antony has been living out, energy is felt to feed back on itself: "Now all labour / Mars what it does; yea, very force entangles / Itself with strength" (4.19.47–49). Appropriately to this, he resolves on suicide only to bungle the attempt. The bathos of this stresses, uncynically, the extent of his demise. In the next scene it is compounded by Cleopatra's refusal to leave the monument to kiss the dying Antony lest she be taken by Caesar. Antony, even as he is trying to transcend defeat by avowing a tragic dignity in death, suffers the indignity of being dragged up the monument.

There is bathos too of course in Caesar's abruptly concluded encomium:

> Hear me, good friends—
> *Enter an Egyptian*
> But I will tell you at some meeter season.
> The business of this man looks out of him.
>
> (5.1.48–50)

The question of Caesar's sincerity here is beside the point; this is, after all, an encomium, and to mistake it for a spontaneous expression of grief will lead us to miss seeing that even in the few moments he speaks Caesar has laid the foundation for an "official" history of Antony. First we are reminded that Caesar *is*—albeit regrettably—the victor. He then vindicates himself and so consolidates that victory by confessing to a humanising grief at the death of his "brother" (though note the carefully placed suggestion of Antony's inferiority: "the *arm* of mine own body"). Caesar further vindicates himself by fatalising events with the by now familiar appeal to necessity, in this case "our stars, / Unreconcilable." Earlier Caesar had told Octavia that "The ostentation of our love . . . left unshown, / Is often left unlov'd" (3.6.52–53). Such is the rationale of his encomium, a strategic expression of "love" in the service of power. The bathos of these episodes makes for an insistent cancelling of the potentially sublime in favour of the political realities which the sublime struggles to eclipse or transcend. Actually, bathos has accompanied Antony throughout, from the very first speech of the play, the last three lines of which are especially revealing (Philo is speaking of Antony):

> Take but good note, and you shall see in him
> The triple pillar of all the world transform'd
> Into a strumpet's fool. Behold and see.
>
> (1.1.11–13)

The cadence of "triple pillar of all the world" arches outward and upward, exactly evoking transcendent aspiration; "transformed" at the line end promises apotheosis; we get instead the jarringly discrepant "strumpet's fool." Cynical, perhaps, but Philo's final terse injunction—"Behold and see"—has prologue-like authority and foresight.

After Antony's death the myth of autonomous *virtus* is shown as finally obsolescent; disentangled now from the prevailing power structure, it survives as legend. Unwittingly Cleopatra's dream about Antony helps relegate him to this realm of the legendary, especially in its use of imagery which is both Herculean and statuesque: "His legs bestrid the ocean; his reared arm / Crested the world" (5.2.82–83). Cleopatra asks Dolabella if such a man ever existed or might exist; he answers: "Gentle Madam, no." Cleopatra vehemently reproaches him only to qualify instantly her own certainty—"But if there be nor ever were one such"—thereby, in the hesitant syntax, perhaps confirming the doubts which prompted the original question.

His legs bestrid the ocean: in dream, in death, Antony becomes at last larger than life; but in valediction is there not also invoked an image of the commemorative statue, that material embodiment of a discourse which, like Caesar's encomium, skilfully overlays (without ever quite obscuring) obsolescence with respect?

HONOUR AND POLICY

If the contradiction which constitutes Antony's identity can be seen as a consequence of a wider conflict between the residual/dominant and the emergent power relations, so too can the strange relationship set up in the play between honour and policy. Pompey's reply to Menas's offer to murder the triumvirs while they are celebrating on board his (Pompey's) galley is a case in point:

> Ah, this thou shouldst have done,
> And not have spoke on't. In me 'tis villainy:
> In thee't had been good service. Thou must know
> 'Tis not my profit that does lead mine honour:
> Mine honour, it. Repent that e'er thy tongue
> Hath so betray'd thine act. Being done unknown,
> I should have found it afterwards well done,
> But must condemn it now.
>
> (2.7.73–80)

Here honour is insisted upon yet divorced from ethics and consequences; the same act is "villainy" or "service" depending on who performs it; ignorance of intent to murder is sufficient condition for approving the murder after the event.

Elsewhere in the play we see these inconsistencies resolved in favour of policy; now honour pretends to integrity—to be thought to possess it is enough. Once again it is a kind of political strategy which takes us back to Machiavelli's *The Prince*. Antony tells Octavia: "If I lose mine honour / I lose myself" (3.4.22–23). Octavia has of course been coerced into marriage with Antony to heal the rift (now re-opened) between him and Caesar, her brother. So, for Antony to speak to her of honour seems hypocritical at least; when, however, Antony goes further and presents himself as the injured party ready nevertheless to forego his revenge in order to indulge Octavia's request that she be *allowed* to act as mediator—"But, as you requested / Yourself shall go between's" (3.4.24–25)—the honour in question is shown to be just another strategy in his continuing exploitation of this woman.

When Thidias is persuading Cleopatra to betray Antony and capitulate to Caesar, honour is now a face-saving strategy for *both* sides; because she "embraced" Antony through fear, says Caesar, he construes the scar upon her honour as "constrained blemishes, / Not as deserv'd." Cleopatra quickly concurs: "He [Caesar] is a god, and knows / What is most right. Mine honour was not yielded, / But conquer'd merely" (3.13.59–62).

In Enobarbus we see how policy aligns positively with realism and judgement. He, like Philo at the outset of the play, Ventidius in act 3, scene 1 and the soldier in act 3, scene 7 who urges Antony not to fight at sea, occupies a role in relation to power very familiar in Jacobean tragedy: he possesses an astuteness characteristic of those removed from, yet involved with and dependent upon—often for their very lives—the centre of power; his is the voice of policy not in the service of aggrandisement so much as a desire for survival. So, for example, we see in act 3, scene 6 Enobarbus attempting to dissuade Cleopatra from participating in the war and Antony from fighting on Caesar's terms. Failing in the attempt, Enobarbus leaves Antony's command but is struck with remorse almost immediately. Since he left without his "chests and treasure" (4.5.8) we are, perhaps, to presume that material gain of this kind was not his motive. Enobarbus, like Antony, comes to embody a contradiction; the speech of his beginning "Mine honesty and I begin to square" (3.13.41) suggests as much, and it becomes clear that he has left his master in the name of the "judgement" which the latter has abdicated but which is integral still to his, Enobarbus's, identity as a soldier. Yet equally integral to that identity is the loyalty which he has betrayed.

The extent of people's dependence upon the powerful is something the play never allows us to forget. Cleopatra's beating of the messenger in act 2, scene 5 is only the most obvious reminder; a subtler and perhaps more effective one comes at the end of the play when Cleopatra attempts to conceal half her wealth from Caesar. In the presence of Caesar she commands Seleucus, her "treasurer," to confirm that she has surrendered all; "speak the truth, Seleucus" she demands and, unfortunately for her he does, revealing that she has kept back as much as she has declared. Cleopatra has ordered him "Upon his *peril*" (5.2.142) to speak the truth (i.e., lie) while he, with an eye to Caesar, replies that he would rather seal his lips "than to my *peril* / Speak that which is not." Here, truth itself is in the service of survival. Cleopatra, outraged, finds this unforgivable; for servants to shift allegiance is, in her eyes (those of a ruler) "base" treachery (5.2.156). The play however, in that ironic repetition of "peril" (my italics) invites an alternative perspective: such a shift is merely a strategy of survival necessitated precisely by rulers like her. Yet doubly ironic is the fact that while Seleucus is described as a "slave, of no more trust / Than love that's hir'd" (5.2.153–54) her own deceit is approved by Caesar as the "wisdom" (5.2.149) appropriate to one in her position. Elsewhere Caesar speaks in passing of the "much tall youth" (2.6.7) that will perish in the event of war; Octavia speaks of the consequence of war between Caesar and Antony being as if "the world should cleave, and that slain men / Should solder up the cleave" (3.4. 31–32; cf. 3.13.180–81; 4.12.41–42; 4.14.17–18). It is a simple yet important truth, one which the essentialist rhetoric is never quite allowed to efface: to kiss away kingdoms is to kiss away also the lives of thousands.

SEXUALITY AND POWER

Those around Antony and Cleopatra see their love in terms of power; languages of possession, subjugation and conspicuous wealth abound in descriptions of the people. More importantly, Antony and Cleopatra actually experience themselves in the same terms. Antony sends Alexas to Cleopatra with the promise that he will "piece / Her opulent throne with kingdoms. All the East / (Say thou) shall call her mistress" (1.5.45–47). Later Caesar describes the ceremony whereby that promise was honoured, a ceremony aiming for an unprecedented *public* display both of wealth and power: "Cleopatra and himself in chairs of gold / Were publicly enthron'd"; Antony gives to Cleopatra the stablishment of Egypt and makes her "Absolute Queen" of Syria, Cyprus and Lydia. "This in the public eye?" inquires Maecenas; "I' th' common showplace" confirms Caesar (3.6.4–12). Cleopatra for her part sends twenty separate messengers to Antony. On his return from Egypt Enobarbus confirms the rumour that eight wild boars were served at a breakfast of only twelve people, adding: "This was but as a fly by an eagle: we had much more monstrous matter of feast, which *worthily deserved noting*" (2.2.185, my italics).

Right from the outset we are told that power is internal to the relationship itself: Philo tells us that Antony has been subjugated by Cleopatra (1.1.1–9) while Enobarbus tells Agrippa that Cleopatra has "pursed up" (ie. pocketed, taken possession of) Antony's heart (2.2.190). As if in a discussion of political strategy, Cleopatra asks Charmian which tactics she should adopt in order to manipulate Antony most effectively. Charmian advocates a policy of complete capitulation; Cleopatra replies: "Thou teachest like a fool—the way to lose him!" (1.3.10). Antony enters and Cleopatra tells him: "I have no power upon you," only then to cast him in the role of treacherous subject: "O, never was there queen / So mightily betrayed. Yet at the first / I saw the treasons planted" (1.3.23–26). Whatever the precise sense of Cleopatra's famous lines at the end of this scene—"O my oblivion is a very Antony, / And I am all forgotten"—there is no doubt that they continue the idea of a power struggle: her extinction is coterminous with his triumph.

Attempting to atone for his departure, Antony pledges himself as Cleopatra's "soldier-servant, making peace or war / As thou affects" (1.3.70). This is just one of many exchanges which shows how their sexuality is rooted in a fantasy transfer of power from the public to the private sphere, from the battlefield to the bed. In act 2, scene 5 Cleopatra recalls with merriment a night of revelry when she subjugated Antony and then engaged in cross-dressing with him, putting "my tires and mantles on him, whilst / I wore his sword Phillipan" (2.5.22–23). Inseparable from the playful reversal of sexual roles is her appropriation of his power, military and sexual, symbolised phallically of course in the sword. Later Antony takes up the sword-power motif in a bitter reproach of Cleopatra for her power over him; here he sees her as his "conqueror" (3.11.66, and cf. 4.14.22–23). Another aspect of the power-sexuality conjunction is suggested in the shamelessly phallic imagery which the lovers use: "Ram thou thy fruitful tidings in mine ears, / That long time have been barren" (2.5.24–25), although again Cleopatra delights in reversing the roles (as at 2.5.10–15).

Here then is another aspect of the contradiction which defines Antony: his sexuality is informed by the very power relations which he, ambivalently, is prepared to sacrifice for sexual freedom; correspondingly, the heroic *virtus* which he wants to reaffirm in and through Cleopatra is in fact almost entirely a function of the power structure which he, again ambivalently, is prepared to sacrifice for her.

Ecstasy there is in this play but not the kind that constitutes a self-sufficient moment above history; if *Antony and Cleopatra* celebrates anything it is not the love which transcends power but the sexual infatuation which foregrounds it. That infatuation is complex: ecstatic, obsessive, dangerous. Of all the possible kinds of sexual encounter, infatuation is perhaps the most susceptible to power—not just because typically it stems from and intensifies an insecurity which often generates possessiveness and its corollary, betrayal, but because it legitimates a free play of self-destructive desire. In Antony's case it is a desire which attends and compensates for the loss of power, a desire at once ecstatic and masochistic and playing itself out in the wake of history, the dust of the chariot wheel.

Enter a Messenger

Laura Quinney

> *All their words are like coals of fire.*
> PIRKE AVOTH

For a long stretch of *Antony and Cleopatra*—until the battle at Actium, late in act 3—Antony's presence in the play is curiously pervasive but abbreviated. He appears in only half the scenes, and, while Cleopatra appears in even fewer, he seems particularly elusive, since so many of the scenes from which he is absent concern his absence itself. As long as he shuttles ambivalently between Rome and Egypt, the question of his whereabouts remains crucial, and a puzzle. Caesar, Pompey, and Cleopatra all spend their time waiting for him and thinking on him. They speculate on his doings with more or less frustration and anxiety. They invoke his name with more or less respect, affection, and resentment. The host of these apostrophes to Antony both make his presence pervasive, and, with their epitaphic drive, imperil it. When he does appear on stage (the first scene excepted), he seems composed and capable, at once too solid and too vulnerable a figure for the demanding investment in him that others have manifested in their apostrophes. The surprising modesty of his grandeur carries over into the ease and the equanimity of his discourse. He is almost equally comfortable in proclaiming his love, parleying at a diplomatic summit, and quibbling at a drinking bout. While Antony is still a pillar of the world, his language shares in the contented dexterity of his power. But after his fall at Actium—from which point, until his death, he dominates the stage—his language suddenly comes into a range and an urgency that it

---

had not had, at the same time that he comes into a fragility prophesied by the other characters' insistent apostrophes to him. His language escapes from subordination and utility when he becomes tenuous to himself, and it becomes tenuous to him.

With Antony's defeat at Actium, his word loses performative power, as he is the first to remark: "Leave me, I pray, a little: pray you now, / Nay, do so; for indeed I have lost command, / Therefore I pray you" (3.11.22–24). Now that his political sovereignty has disintegrated, he cannot issue commands, but can only, like the powerless and outcast, beg that his small, privative requests should be heard and respected. Yet at the end of this scene, his language claims for itself a performative power more comprehensive than an emperor's: "Fall not a tear, I say; one of them rates / All that is won and lost" (ll. 69–70). The performative power that Antony's language assumes here is of a different order from that which he has forfeited. This power is as ungrounded as it is expansive—language affirming itself in the absence of the subject's empirical authority. And Antony is himself moved by this transformation in his relationship to his own language. With "Fall not a tear, I say," his mood changes utterly; the spirit of shame, anguish, and recrimination dissolves, and in its place rises quiet acceptance: "Give me a kiss; / Even this repays me" (ll. 70–71).

He seems to step into the stride and assurance of his language; and yet his anxiety emerges as his language flares. These lines express, after all, the pathos of life and desire constricted to the smallest scope—to a tear, a kiss. The pathos of such a minimalism lingers as Antony struggles toward the soothing surface of activity; he wavers between pursuing the continuity of mundane life, and attending to the absorbing heaviness of his spirit: "We sent our schoolmaster: / Is a come back? Love, I am full of lead. / Some wine, within there, and our viands!" (ll. 71–73). His anxiety is here strangely coterminous with the exuberance of his language, as if this exuberance sprung from, but also sustained, his sense of dislocation. Antony's political displacement results in his displacement from his own language; and his language then reveals, not a perfect autonomy from him as the speaking subject, but an alterity that makes it at once distant and free. With "Fall not a tear, I say," Antony can be both affirmative and sad, because he has here discovered the impotent generosity of language.

This is the discovery, and the life, given to those whom "Fortune" has abandoned. The play is littered with the casualties of imperial conflict and consolidation; and when they lose their political viability, these preterite figures turn to seek in language the elusive space of their survival. In this space there emerges what Maurice Blanchot, in his book *L'Entretien infini*, calls "the other rapport," a rapport with that impersonality and impossibility whose existence is obscured by power and place. That Antony's relationship to his language should change in this way is prefigured by Pompey's brief appearance. An early and easy casualty of the battle over the empire, Pompey suffers for his fatal incompetence with the ways and the rhetoric of imperial powerplay. He may claim nobility for his purposes in a bold and censurious speech (2.6.8–22), and he may scoff at the compromise the triumvirate has offered him (ll. 34–39), but all this brave rhetoric is vitiated when he sheepishly concedes, "Know then / I came before you here a man prepared / To take this offer" (ll. 40–41). His rhetoric is characteristically more sovereign than it can justify; he pitches it high, but he wears it ill. Caesar observes coldly, "Since I saw you last / There's a change upon you," to which Pompey retorts, "Well, I know not / What counts harsh fortune casts upon my face, / But in my bosom shall she never come / To make my heart her vassal" (ll. 51–56). Though valiant, his words are sadly untrue, since his despair has already caused him to "laugh away his fortune" (l. 105), as Menas bitterly remarks. Pompey's high rhetoric collapses, because his situation and his spirit cannot sustain it. His naive and uneasy handling of rhetoric, like his residual attachment to "honor," make him a doomed anachronism.

At his entrance, then, the play encourages us to take Pompey for an awkward and empty boaster. Yet when Pompey falls to his weakest, after he dismisses his last chance for power, and so guarantees his disappearance from the political arena, as from the play, he suddenly steps into the stride of language. At the climax of the boisterous celebration on his galley, this figure, shadowed by defeat and coming extinction, suddenly speaks out with urgency and longing: "O, Antony, / You have my father's house. But what, we are friends!" (2.7.130). With its (not unambivalent) burst of generosity, and its undercurrent of forlorn appeal, this line seeks a new rapport, outside the domain of diplomacy and imperialism. Aspiring to an intimacy for which there is no room, it becomes the refuge of Pompey's life, at the same time that it confines his life to this (last) moment of language.

In the final soliloquies of Enobarbus—who follows Pompey in homoerotic mourning for Antony—this changed relationship to language becomes even more vividly opulent and hopeless. Enobarbus speaks these soliloquies as a shunned pariah, not to be mentioned again, nor mourned himself. His position of utter loss transforms the character of his language; it loses the balance of shrewd, rational appraisal, and becomes, instead, expansive and supplicating. Enobarbus is moved and grieved by Antony's unexpected generosity to him; it is not only unwarranted, but an instance of that noble excess in Antony, which allows him to go on "o'erflowing the measure" even after he has been stripped. "Your emperor / Continues still a Jove" (4.6.28–29), as the soldier says, who brings Enobarbus's treasure, with Antony's "bounty overplus." Now that he has been stripped to his word, Enobarbus finds a similarly impossible excess, and repays Antony in the only means at his disposal—the wealth of hyperbole: "O Antony, / Thou mine of bounty, how wouldst thou have paid / My better service, when my turpitude / Thou dost so crown with gold" (ll. 31–34). Antony's bounty overflows into the generosity of Enobarbus's language. At the very end, his comparisons break from symmetry: "O Antony, / Nobler than my revolt is infamous / Forgive me in thine own particular" (4.9.18–20). When the space and time of Enobarbus's life shrink to that of his language, he invests it with the urgency and power of action, or, as Blanchot puts it in "La Mésure, le suppliant," "lorsqu'il y a défaut de tout, l'homme abîme dans le malheur est en mésure de parler, car c'est-là sa vraie mésure." But the expansiveness of his language strays from Enobarbus himself, and his apostrophes go unheard by the one to whom they appeal; despite the vocabulary of "wealth" and "payment" used here, the phenomenon described is not an economic or compensatory one. The space of the subject reduced to the word becomes a space of isolation and futility.

Much of the sadness in *Antony and Cleopatra* arises from Antony's gradual reduction to this space. In the climactic departure of Hercules, for example, the spirit of Antony's isolation materializes. On the night before battle, his soldiers on watch hear a supernatural, fading music whose mystery troubles them. They huddle together, anxiously wondering, "What should this mean?" until one among them declares grimly, "'Tis the god Hercules, whom Antony loved / Now leaves him" (4.3.14–16). The soldiers' anxiety and fatalism spill over from Antony's own, which he had manifested in the crisis pitch of the previous scene. There, in a flushed and restive mood, he makes an elaborate farewell to his servants. His sense of his own deterioration, both in fortune and in psychological integrity, stirs him to this gratuitous and extravagant gesture. In the grip of his apprehension, Antony feels an aura of fatality envelop him, out of which he can appeal to his servants, to cherish and secure this ghost of him still living: "Tend me tonight: May be it is the period of your duty. / Haply you shall not see me more: or if, /A mangled shadow. . . . I look on you / As one that takes his leave" (4.2.23–29). He feels himself to be so abstracted, so insubstantial that he is already fading from the world, his presence more tenuous not only than his servants', but than that of the "mangled shadow" to be memorialized in the alien imperviousness of death. And yet only in these other presences can Antony find an intimation of his own attenuated self, as if he were a figure in a mirror seeking a body to reflect. He enters into such a specular relationship with his own language when it seems to harbor in itself the "I" fast fading from him: "I look on you as one that takes his leave." His anxiety, which is coterminous with this sense of himself as residualized and isolated, overflows from the one scene to the next, where it conjures up the sadness of departing music, and where that departure certifies the emergence of the other rapport.

The spirit of abandonment in this scene colors the rest of the play. Hercules' departure underscores a transition recognized by everyone, including Antony and Cleopatra: history belongs to Caesar, and to them belongs only a space of time and of language. Antony and Cleopatra are acutely aware of surviving into this limbo, where they sustain themselves at preternatural length. Hercules' abandonment is, oddly enough, followed by a temporary upswing in Antony's fortunes— his one thriving day of battle—and by Antony and Cleopatra's tenderest moments. But the spirit of abandonment has so touched the play that this ephemeral success seems "wild"—a grace as exuberant as it is fragile and surprising.

This is the sense in which Antony and Cleopatra take their victory. Antony understands his single triumph to be so much against the trend of history that his celebration of it leaps to apocalyptic terms: "Trumpeters, / With brazen din blast you the city's ear, / Make mingle with our rattling tambourines, / That heaven and earth may strike their sounds together, / Applauding our approach" (4.8.35–39). In their victory Antony and Cleopatra take a joy as buoyant and fleeting as the victory was wild. Their intimate moments become unassuming and gentle in the light of this fragility. They wake up in bed, and Cleopatra helps Antony dress for battle, while he tries to share his proud excitement: "O, love, / That thou could'st see my wars today, and knew'st / The royal occupation: thou should'st see / A workman in't" (4.4.15–18). The sweetness of these moments arises from the fragility in which

Antony and Cleopatra now live, the fragility of the world formed in the moment of language. Thus their sadness lingers at the height of celebration. Cleopatra greets Antony, returning triumphant from battle, with these dark, joyous words: "O Lord of lords, / O infinite virtue, com'st thou smiling from / The world's great snare uncaught?" and Antony replies in the same cadences of haunted affirmation, "Mine nightingale, / We have beat them to their beds. What, girl! Though gray / Do something mingle with our younger brown" (4.8.17–20). In their isolation, signified by the withdrawal of a listening god, the space of their lives turns to words, at the same time that words, now the locus of the other rapport, open out only to absence.

For Antony, language comes to harbor a confidence like the lost substantiality of the self, but at a distance infinitely remote. This is its generosity, the source of affirmation in the play, and its limitation, the source of tragic affect. This generosity emerges as if it were a movement in language answering to the survival of Antony's "heart." "Heart" should carry here its full Shakespearean resonance, so that it means not only courage and affection, but the spirit from which these spring, the residue of the self that perseveres in a buoyant autonomy from its worldly fate. It is a center that, after Actium, is continually displaced in Antony, which he is always seeking, and which is always eluding his grasp. In his language he hears the recovery of his "heart," though, harbored there, it remains elusive and estranged. He invokes this distant echo when, recovering from his bout with Thidias, he asks, "Where hast thou been, my heart?" (3.13.171), and when he tells Cleopatra, helping him arm for battle, "Ah, let be, let be. Thou art / The armorer of my heart" (4.4.6–7). Because it seems as displaced from him as his own heart, his language can offer him its failed generosity. When he has reached the ebb of loss, where he feels himself to be as attenuated and amorphous as a cloud, even then his words take on an assurance far removed from his own experience of disintegration: "My good knave Eros, now thy captain is / Even such a body: here I am Antony, / Yet cannot hold this visible shape, my knave" (4.14.12–14). In offering Antony all the impersonal resources of its wealth and assurance, his language responds to, but does not answer, his own experience of attenuation; the remote alterity of language only makes it more acutely felt. This alterity is dramatized not only in Antony's changed relationship to his words, but in his changed relationship to the play's messengers and messenger-figures.

II

Antony and Cleopatra includes a startling number of messages and messengers. In *The Common Liar,* Janet Adelman points out that among the dramatis personae there are eight nameless "messengers" and another seven characters who act primarily as messengers (Alexas, Varrius, Thidias, Mardian, Proculeius, Dolabella, and Antony's schoolmaster). To their number I would add what I call the "messenger-figures": the Soothsayer, Diomedes, and the Clown. The play's central conflicts— which lie in the characters' imperialist struggles and psychological ambivalence—are represented in terms of the manipulation and treatment of messengers. They are spurned, beaten, sent to lie, and sent to ensnare. They bear news that, whether galling or welcome, rapidly turns obsolete in the flux of ambivalence and powerplay. Yet in the course of *Antony and Cleopatra*, the role of the messenger is so transformed that this figure comes to have its own thematic. The messengers begin as messengers, but end as angelloi; they are at first merely representatives, but, for Antony at least, they finally develop an autonomous presence, ushering in a rapport that is anonymous and otherworldly. Standing on the threshold between subject and language, they are not quite characters, not psyches, yet they have autonomous will and feeling. Because they maintain this liminal position, they can exemplify the quasi-human, but impersonal and anonymous traits of the alterity of language—its generosity, intimacy, and distance.

To Caesar and his messenger-agents belongs the sterile impersonality of the bureaucrat. Caesar adopts the role of a faceless and efficient administrator, who consolidates his power by skillfully deploying a legion of methodical operatives. This political style originates in, and fulfills, Caesar's brilliant imperialist imagination, by which Antony is scourged and defeated, as it is, in turn, a symptom of Antony's failure that he should find the other anonymity in his rapport with the messenger. Unlike Antony, Caesar pursues a canny utilitarianism in his relationship to the messengers. His opening scene dramatizes this relationship, when an envoy enters to assure him, "Thy biddings have been done, and every hour, / Most noble Caesar, shalt thou have report / How 'tis abroad" (1.4.34–36). Through a network of messengers which operates as an information police, Caesar supervises the terrain of expanding empire and accelerating political conflict. In this panoptical extension of himself, he is made preternaturally ubiquitous, disseminated across myriad points of reconnaissance, along which, "every hour," the news flies.

Caesar knows this self-dissemination to be the principle of his radical, ineluctable ascendency. In his climactic encounter with Octavia, returning from her brief marriage, Caesar rises to a curious and telling moment of energy in his customarily dry speech. He is unusually excited throughout this scene, rather cruelly insisting to his sister, despite her own attempts to maintain dignity, that she is Antony's "castaway," "an abstract 'tween his lust and him," an abandoned wife who has had to enter Rome like "a market maid" (3.6.40, 61, 51). Though happy to reappropriate his beloved Octavia, Caesar thrills even more to find that, with Antony's misbehavior, he is free to unleash his own imperial designs, as well as his primal hatred for "our great competitor." But he is most energized to recall the means and assurance of his triumph, when he presses Octavia by saying, "Where is [Antony] now?" and declares with a sinister confidence:

> I have eyes upon him,
> And his affairs come to me upon the wind.
> (3.6.62–63)

This moment proves so keen for the temperate Caesar because in it he experiences the nature of his own power—as a man all eyes, an impersonal intelligence that ranges as if supernaturally diffused and incorporeal. He is the spirit of bureaucratic anonymity—invisible, ubiquitous, omniscient—that has dissolved into a racing, multifarious power. The play corroborates this view of Caesar, and reproduces his excitement, when it has him advance on Antony and Cleopatra with the speed of a superhuman and selfless force. News of his swift course reaches Antony and his generals, stirring in them a worried confusion over this antagonist who is strangely nebulous yet saturating: "This speed of Caesar's / Carries beyond belief." "Can he be there in person? 'Tis impossible; / Strange that his power should be." "While he was yet in Rome / His power went out in such distractions as / Beguiled all spies" (3.7.74–75, 56–57, 75–77). The play represents Caesar as uninhibited by temporal and spatial constraints, unlike Antony and Cleopatra, because his power is not located in him, but diffused among proxies.

Caesar's political style speeds the rise of imperialism, where Antony and Cleopatra's faith in charisma and personal loyalty suffers the fate of a static anachronism. The cult of charismatic personality falters more and more miserably, until it finally lapses into such ineffectual challenges as Antony's demand for single fight ("His coin, ships, legions / May be a coward's, whose ministers would prevail / Under the service of a child as soon as Caesar. I dare him therefore" [3.13.20–22]). In his archaic attachment to personal nobility, Antony does not see that Caesar has triumphed precisely because he has abandoned individualism, and established the rule of the "ministers"; his empire waxes strong on the structural solidity of a power network efficient unto itself, and so appropriate for the maintenance of a vast, disparate territory. Antony and Cleopatra are defeated in the same way by Caesar's imperialist mode of articulating politics and representation. Caesar designs and exploits the propagandistic value of documentation and "shows" in which he effaces himself, while drawing others into his chosen representation of history. Meanwhile, Antony and Cleopatra produce themselves as theatrical spectacle, a display that goes to demonstrate their personal distinction and to reaffirm the status quo. "Show me, my women, like a queen" (5.2.227), Cleopatra proclaims, where Caesar harps on "What I can show in this" ("this" being his innocence in Antony's death; [5.1.77]). The conflict between these two modes of political theatre finally culminates in the specter of Caesar's triumphal pageant—a propagandistic drama of imperialist enslavement which Antony and Cleopatra regard in the light of the most acute personal humiliation.

Yet because Caesar makes such productive use of his "ministers" and "representatives," he would not recognize, and his proxies do not in fact develop, the autonomous presence and the other anonymity that attends on Antony, when he encounters the more gravely marginalized and powerless of the messenger-figures. For this reason, the play's most elaborate messenger scene—Antony's tantrum at Thidias—does not participate in the disjunctive rhythms of the other messenger scenes. As a purposeful representative of Caesar, Thidias is easily drawn into the pattern of identification and ambivalence which causes Antony to lash out at him. Uncanniness only arises in the angelloi, those orphaned and otherworldly figures invisible in the blaze of power.

In the play's first scene, the messengers appear as the intrusive agents of Caesar, as ciphers for his summons to legal duty and obligation. Antony treats them as vexatious reminders, and impatiently spurns them, as if that were to escape what they represent. The agitation that their appearance excites in him he projects outward, into the apocalyptic collapse of this intrusive world, against which he can then contrast, and renew, his imaginary refuge: "Let Rome in Tiber

melt, and the wide arch / Of the ranged empire fall! Here is my space"
(1.1.33–34). The space of this delicate idyll would be one in which
messengers could mediate intimacy, not empire, and imperial rulers
could become anonymous flaneurs:

> Fie, wrangling queen!
> Whom everything becomes—to chide, to laugh,
> To weep; whose every passion fully strives
> To make itself, in thee, fair and admired.
> No messenger but thine; and all alone
> Tonight we'll wander through the streets and note
> The qualities of people. Come, my queen;
> Last night you did desire it. [*To Attendants*] Speak not to us.
> *Exeunt Antony and Cleopatra with the Train.*
>
> (1.1.49–55)

In Plutarch, Antony and Cleopatra actually do disguise themselves
as ordinary people, and go to mingle with the crowds in the streets of
Alexandria. But Shakespeare recasts this activity in the mode of "desire," of a daydream in which their intimacy could have the oblivion it
is not allowed in the play: the two never appear "all alone," but are
always accompanied and observed by an audience of waiting-women,
eunuchs, generals, and so on. Even after this speech, with its appeal to
privacy, and its rebuff, "Speak not to us," Antony and Cleopatra are
in their sweeping exit encircled by "the Train." The wish for a private
intimacy remains a fantasy because it is not, in fact, true to the style of
Antony and Cleopatra. They are regal figures who thrive on public
admiration, and who do not distinguish between political and intimate
life, which they subject to the same project of self-dramatization.
Antony can exact the wonder of a universal audience even in this scene
("I bind / On pain of punishment, the world to weet / We stand up
peerless" [37–39]), and can imagine such an attentive public even in the
shadowiness and impersonality of the underworld ("Where souls do
couch on flowers, we'll hand in hand, / And with our sprightly port
make the ghosts gaze" [4.14.51–52]).

Like the first, the second scene also involves the repudiation of
messages. Here, Charmian and Iras make bawdy of the Soothsayer's
enigmatic prophecies. Removed from the action, blank of character
and history, the Soothsayer is the pure spirit of the messenger, a
remote and grave presence imbued with the anonymous wisdom of the
otherworldly. He is the most emblematic of the messenger-figures

who, early on, reveal their capacity for chilling detachment and the strangely impersonal intimacy it makes possible. But because these figures are as yet anomalous, their audience now either overlooks or, shaken, retreats from their preternatural austerity.

The Soothsayer's appearance works to cast an aura of uncanniness over the messenger-figure, as we feel a few moments later, when Antony determines to hear the envoys he had shunned in the previous scene. The first messenger is talkative and sympathetic, but the second is terse and dark. He materializes suddenly, in answer to the call for news "From Sicyon." Looking up from a distracted meditation, Antony gasps, "What are you?" (1.2.117), as if this nameless functionary had a piercing air. The messenger replies starkly:

> Fulvia thy wife is dead.
>
> (1.2.118)

He ignores Antony's question, and omits the softening speeches of his predecessor. Handing Antony a letter, the messenger adds, as if it were the power of his impersonal office to fathom all priorities and needs, "Her length of sickness, with what else more serious / Importeth thee to know, this bears" (ll. 120–21). His distant and austere familiarity fulfills the promise of uncanniness in Antony's spellbound "What are you?"

This intimacy can be paradoxically remote and impersonal because it arises between a subject and a spirit void of a subject. In the first half of the play, this anonymous spirit makes its most dramatic approach with the second and final appearance of the Soothsayer, this time before Antony. The Soothsayer opens with the same disjunctive and terse severity as the messenger from Sicyon:

> ANTONY. Now, sirrah, you do wish yourself in Egypt?
> SOOTHSAYER. Would I had never come from thence, nor
>   you thither.
>
> (2.3.11)

He is empowered to speak with a disinterested authority and candor. His prophecy can claim that it is closer to Antony's fate than Antony himself, and can describe this fate with an accuracy as grim as it is rigorous: "Thy daemon, that thy spirit which keeps thee, is / Noble, courageous, high, unmatchable, / Where Caesar's is not. But near him thy angel becomes afeard, as being o'erpowered: therefore / Make space enough between you" (ll. 19–24). But there is no masterful subject behind this knowledge and assurance. The Soothsayer's grandly precise and dispassionate rhetoric produces its own spirit of austerity; and the anonymous figures who speak this rhetoric, the figures whose dramatic lives work only to speak it, diffuse the chilling aura of this language. The Soothsayer and the messenger from Sicyon appear as uncanny presences not only because they speak a cold message in cold words, but because they uncannily assume the character of these words; they enter not as subjects, who can command or fail to command their own language, but as the impersonal spirit of that language itself. At this point, Antony himself recoils from such a strange phenomenon; he hurries the second messenger out with "Forebear me," while he anxiously tells the Soothsayer "Speak this no more," and "Get thee gone."

In the play's first scene, the messengers appear as an encroaching public, whose intervention stirs Antony to an illusive wish for anonymity; but when Antony's fortunes have irrevocably deteriorated, he will find the spirit of anonymous intimacy in the messenger figures. The change in Antony's relationship to the messengers comes just after the battle at Actium, in the scene immediately following Antony's speech, "Fall not a tear, I say," with its appeal to the generosity of language. A representative appears at Caesar's camp to bargain for the lives of Antony and Cleopatra. Having never encountered this lowly subject of his new empire, Caesar must ask, "Know you him?" and Dolabella tartly identifies him as Antony's schoolmaster, "An argument that he is plucked, when hither / He sends so poor a pinion of his wing, / Which had superfluous kings for messengers / Not many moons gone by" (3.12.1–6). Dolabella takes the relative anonymity and unimportance of the messenger to indicate a poverty in Antony. When the schoolmaster enters, he seems to corroborate this view, but what he says in fact completely reverses its tenor and affect. This "poor," unknown figure speaks in a first person which is peacefully emptied out; his is the fidelity of the insignificant and anonymous, free to affirm Antony's "bounty" as if it still continued into the present:

> Such as I am, I come from Antony.
> I was of late as petty to his ends
> As is the morn-dew on the myrtle leaf
> To his grand sea.
>
> (3.12.7–10)

With the quiet expansiveness of these lines, the messenger becomes more than a messenger, though still less than a subject; he becomes the spirit of an impersonal intimacy waiting on the "heart" in Antony that survives his worldly decay. His generosity springs from the groundless exuberance of his language, just as this exuberance itself resembles the generosity of an insignificant and anonymous person. Out of Antony's entry into the alterity of language, there materializes this messenger who, unlike his predecessors, is not austere, but gifted with the impersonal kindness and generosity of the other rapport.

When Antony falls to his lowest ebb, he can welcome the alterity of this intimate distance, and can requite the grave generosity of the messenger. After Eros foils Antony's suicide, Antony's own guard flees from him in panic and dismay. Only Decretas pauses long enough to steal the bloody sword which he hopes will "enter" him with Caesar, and he is so furtive in this opportunism that he ignores Diomedes' question, "Lives he? / Wilt thou not answer, man?" (4.14.115). Antony's dying seems destined to take place amid hysteria, betrayal, and then lonely silence. He has been left wretchedly begging to be dispatched when Diomedes enters, fulfilling the wish made long ago for "No messenger but thine." With Diomedes' first words, the atmosphere of the scene changes from anguish to quiet concentration. For with Diomedes enters the spirit of calm and disinterested attentiveness. Antony's exchange with him is pared down to the fewest words, whose weight each knows, so that he speaks with a familiar brevity, as without now superfluous affect:

> DIOMEDES. Most absolute lord,
>   My mistress Cleopatra sent me to thee.
> ANTONY. When did she send thee?
> DIOMEDES. Now, my lord.
> ANTONY. Where is she?
> DIOMEDES. Locked in her monument.
>
> (4.14.116–17)

Diomedes responds to Antony's change of tone without surprise, as Antony responds to his news without anger or bitterness. Stages of feeling are simply ellipsed, as if irrelevant, and the two figures share instead a muted understanding and regret. When Diomedes comes to tell of his mission, he acknowledges its failure, but touches on it as lightly as Antony's mood is quiet. He describes the tragedy he has found with gentle understatement:

> She had a prophesying fear
> Of what hath come to pass; for when she saw
> (Which never shall be found) you did suspect
> She had disposed with Caesar, and that your rage
> Would not be purged, she sent you word she was dead;
> But, fearing since how it might work, hath sent
> Me to proclaim the truth, and I am come,
> I dread, too late.
>
> (4.14.120–26)

This sentence slows to its subdued and careful end. The "and" which introduces the last, grim reflection ("and I am come") mutes the potential for melodrama; no climactic transition is marked, but only a soft fall into the heaviness of "too late." Antony matches the messenger's calm austerity when he confirms and echoes his words, as if in intimate, lyrical refrain:

> and I am come,
> I dread, too late.
> Too late, good Diomed.

This scene, with its unexpected turns of feeling, and its close, elliptical dialogue, takes on the form of an intimate encounter. Antony finds a delicate and evanescent rapport with a figure who, though named, is nonetheless fleeting and anonymous, a creature of the moment of language. (Diomedes has not appeared before, and will appear only once more, to answer Cleopatra's question, "How now? Is he dead?" with a bleak precision: "His death's upon him, but not dead" [4.15.5–6]). The messenger emerges from his utilitarian function, and the anonymity of the functionary, to manifest an autonomous presence and a different kind of anonymity—that of a spirit not human, available only in the mode of an impersonal and distant intimacy displaced from the world, when Antony himself is displaced from it.

But it is with Cleopatra that the play irradiates the alterity of language and its intimacy, for she welcomes this alterity without the mediation of the angelloi, and even more luminously than Antony can ever do. Amid the flux of events, she remains oddly unchanging and removed. Neither her character nor her language undergo the dramatic transformation of Antony's. From her two scenes with the envoy bearing news of Antony's marriage, it is clear that the affect associated with the angelloi already belongs to Cleopatra, in whom it has advanced beyond the influence of messenger figures. She is from the beginning what she will be—the play's most intent and moving speaker, a figure given over to the space of language and the other rapport. Her word has an exuberant solitariness all its own until late in the play—when Antony's joins hers in this, after his collapse at the battle of Actium.

Cleopatra is vigorously self-dramatizing, and correspondingly keen in her awareness of the theatricality of other people's rhetoric. She can puncture Antony's expansive, "Let Rome in Tiber melt," with the tart riposte, "Excellent falsehood!"; and when he attempts to take a stately leave of her, she can mock his high rhetoric: "Good now, play one scene / Of excellent dissembling, and let it look / Like perfect honor" (1.3.75–77). As Anthony Brennan has argued in his essay, "Excellent Dissembling: Antony and Cleopatra Playing at Love," their intimacy involves understanding and responding to one another's self-dramatizations. But the relationship between intimacy and self-dramatization is not unmediated. Cleopatra's language often seems to be pitched above her audience (including us), opening outward as if in appeal to an attention more comprehensive and an intelligence more perfectly sympatico with her production of herself. Such attention and intelligence do not exist; and this appeal to absence gives her language its solitary grandeur. Her frenzied encounter with the messenger bearing news of Antony's marriage ends in such a moment of majestic exile:

> CLEOPATRA. In praising Antony I have dispraised Caesar.
> CHARMIAN. Many times, madam.
> CLEOPATRA. I am paid for't now.
>
> (2.5.107–8)

The grave justice of "I am paid for't now" is not quite addressed to Charmian, but to a disengaged silence and distance. Her language appeals to this other rapport when she says wonderingly, "Though age from folly could not give me freedom, / It does from childishness. Can Fulvia die?" a capacious but enigmatic question elided by Antony's response, "She's dead, my queen" (1.3.58–59). But it is not only in moments of shock or abandonment that her language appeals to the other rapport, for she manifests, from beginning to end, the knowledge of her own stature and isolation. She can address even Antony in words that, though supplicating, seem distracted from him, as if their distance and futility were what he ought to love in her:

> Courteous lord, one word.
> Sir, you and I must part, but that's not it:
> Sir, you and I have loved, but there's not it:
> That you know well. Something it is I would—
> O, my oblivion is a very Antony,
> And I am all forgotten.
>
> (1.3.86–91)

This speech is strangely aware of a remoteness from its listener, and a solitary communication with the elusive spirit of a nonhuman intelligence. This sense of her world's isolation allows Cleopatra to speak, when she wishes to, with the precision and austerity of the messengers, as when she asks Antony, "Not know me yet?" or replies to Caesar's "I'll take my leave" with the bracing truth, "And may, through all the world: 'tis yours" (5.2.133–34).

It may seem odd that, with its distance and difficulty, her question, "Not know me yet?" should appear in the play's most commanding representation of intimacy, in the moment of intense conference after Antony's violent attack on Thidias.

> ANTONY. To flatter Caesar, would you mingle eyes
>   With one that ties his points?
> CLEOPATRA. Not know me yet?
> ANTONY. Cold-hearted toward me?
>
> (3.12.156–58)

This dialogue has the antiphonal rhythm and elliptical expression of an intimate exchange, but it is also oddly disjunctive. With their brave solitude, the words of Antony and Cleopatra join the elliptical expression of intimacy and the isolation of language opening out to the other rapport. Here, to be humanly intimate means to be moved by the anonymous intimacy of the other's language.

Cleopatra's "last conquest" takes this form of intimacy, when she brings Dolabella to speak a language that corresponds to her own in heroic sincerity, and corresponds to it especially because he denies her words, when she herself knows this denial to be just:

> CLEOPATRA. Think you there was or might be such a man
>   As this I dreamt of?
> DOLABELLA. Gentle madam, no.
>
> (5.2.92–93)

It testifies to the summoning power of Cleopatra's poetry that she can make this agent of the clammy Caesar emerge into the austerity and distant familiarity of the angelloi. In this context, Stephen Booth has engagingly argued that the actor playing Antony doubled for Dolabella. Whether or not Booth's claim is accurate, his view illuminates this moment: the intimacy between Antony and Cleopatra here resurfaces uncannily as a rapport touched by the spirit of the angelloi, and mediated by the remote alterity of language.

The absent rapport summoned up by the rhetorical power of Cleopatra's language constantly makes us feel the impoverishment of the play's world, with its incorrigible binary oppositions and its stingy imperialist ethos, just as the generosity of her language produces the sense of buoyant affirmation in the play. Critics generally try to say what is being affirmed, whether it is a mystical union of love and death (Knight), the imaginative vision of love (Adelman), or the creation of private value (Eagleton). But the sense of affirmation comes first from Antony and Cleopatra's language, before an object of affirmation can be found. The solitariness of Cleopatra's language is, curiously enough, not bleak, but the source of an exuberance which gives sweep and buoyancy even to speeches whose content is not altogether happy, like "My salad days . . ." (1.4.73–end), and even to those spoken at the bleakest moments: "O sun, / Burn the great sphere thou mov'st in: darkling stand / The varying shore of the world. O Antony / Antony, Antony!" (4.15.9–12). From the beginning, Cleopatra knows and loves this impotent generosity of language—which explains the strange tonality of the last act, with its leisurely pace and its strange, erotic happiness. In this act, which Cleopatra has all to herself, she can receive with perfect equanimity the most fantastic of the messenger-figures, a peasant bearing the asps and the eerie salutation, "I wish you joy o'th'worm" (5.2.279); and can free her words, with their call elsewhere, to the most startling affirmations: "go fetch / My best attires. I am again for Cydnus, / To meet Mark Antony" (5.2.226–28).

Chronology

1564   William Shakespeare born at Stratford-on-Avon to John Shakespeare, a butcher, and Mary Arden. He is baptized on April 26.

1582   Marries Anne Hathaway in November.

1583   Daughter Susanna born, baptized on May 26.

1585   Twins Hamnet and Judith born, baptized on February 2.

1588–90   Sometime during these years, Shakespeare goes to London, without family. First plays performed in London.

1590–92   *The Comedy of Errors*, the three parts of *Henry VI.*

1593–94   Publication of *Venus and Adonis* and *The Rape of Lucrece*, both dedicated to the Earl of Southampton. Shakespeare becomes a sharer in the Lord Chamberlain's company of actors. *The Taming of the Shrew, The Two Gentlemen of Verona, Richard III, Titus Andronicus.*

1595–97   *Romeo and Juliet, Richard II, King John, A Midsummer Night's Dream, Love's Labor's Lost.*

1596   Son Hamnet dies. Grant of arms to father.

1597   *The Merchant of Venice, Henry IV, Part 1.* Purchases New Place in Stratford.

1598–1600   *Henry IV, Part 2, As You Like It, Much Ado about Nothing, Twelfth Night, The Merry Wives of Windsor, Henry V,* and *Julius Caesar.* Moves his company to the new Globe Theatre.

1601   *Hamlet.* Shakespeare's father dies, buried on September 8.

1601–2   *Troilus and Cressida.*

1603   Death of Queen Elizabeth; James VI of Scotland becomes James I of England; Shakespeare's company becomes the King's Men.

1603–4   *All's Well That Ends Well, Measure for Measure, Othello.*

1605–6   *King Lear, Macbeth.*

1607   Marriage of daughter Susanna on June 5.

1607–8   *Timon of Athens, Antony and Cleopatra, Pericles, Coriolanus.*

1608   Shakespeare's mother dies, buried on September 9.

1609   *Cymbeline*, publication of sonnets. Shakespeare's company purchases Blackfriars Theatre.

1610–11   *The Winter's Tale, The Tempest.* Shakespeare retires to Stratford.

1612–13   *Henry VIII, Two Noble Kinsmen.*

1616   Marriage of daughter Judith on February 10. Shakespeare dies at Stratford on April 23.

1623   Publication of the Folio edition of Shakespeare's plays.

Contributors

HAROLD BLOOM, Sterling Professor of the Humanities at Yale University, is the author of *The Anxiety of Influence, Poetry and Repression,* and many other volumes of literary criticism. His forthcoming study, *Freud: Transference and Authority,* attempts a full-scale reading of all of Freud's major writings. A MacArthur Prize Fellow, he is general editor of five series of literary criticism published by Chelsea House. During 1987–88, he served as Charles Eliot Norton Professor of Poetry at Harvard University.

JANET ADELMAN is Professor of English at the University of California, Berkeley. She is the author of *The Common Liar: An Essay on Antony and Cleopatra,* as well as several articles on Shakespeare and Milton.

ANNE BARTON is Professor of English at Cambridge University. She is the author of *Shakespeare and the Idea of the Play* and *Ben Jonson, Dramatist,* and is one of the editors of The Riverside Shakespeare.

ROSALIE L. COLIE was Professor of English at Brown University until her death in 1972. She is the author of *Paradoxia Epidemica: The Resources of Kind, Shakespeare's Living Art,* and *Atlantic Wall and Other Poems.*

HOWARD FELPERIN is Professor of English at Melbourne University, Australia. His books include *Shakespearean Romance, Shakespearean Representation,* and *Beyond Deconstruction: The Uses and Abuses of Literary Theory.*

JOHN BAYLEY is Thomas Wharton Professor of English Literature at Oxford University. His books include *The Uses of Division, Selected Essays, Romantic Survival, Shakespeare and Tragedy,* and *Pushkin: A Comparative Commentary.*

LINDA BAMBER is Associate Professor of English at Tufts University.

JONATHAN DOLLIMORE is Lecturer in English at the University of Sussex. He is the author of *Radical Tragedy* and coeditor of *Political Shakespeare*.

LAURA QUINNEY is a member of the Society of Fellows, Harvard University. She is working on a critical study of Samuel Johnson.

Bibliography

Bamber, Linda. *Comic Women, Tragic Men*. Stanford, Calif.: Stanford University Press, 1982.

Barnet, Sylvan. "Recognition and Reversal in *Antony and Cleopatra*." *Shakespeare Quarterly* 8 (1957): 331–34.

Baroll, J. Leeds. *Artificial Persons*. Columbia: University of South Carolina Press, 1974.

Barton, Anne. *Shakespeare and the Idea of the Play*. London: Chatto & Windus, 1961.

Bayley, John. *Shakespeare and Tragedy*. London: Routledge & Kegan Paul, 1981.

Bono, Barbara J. *Literary Transvaluation: From Vergilian Epic to Shakespearean Tragicomedy*. Berkeley and Los Angeles: University of California Press, 1984.

Bowers, John M. " 'I am Marble-Constant': Cleopatra's Monumental End." *Huntington Library Quarterly* 46, no. 4 (1983): 283–97.

Bradbrook, Muriel C. *Themes and Contentions of Elizabethan Tragedy*. Cambridge: Cambridge University Press, 1979.

Bradley, Andrew C. *Shakespearean Tragedy*. London: Macmillan, 1915.

Brennan, Anthony S. "Excellent Dissembling: Antony and Cleopatra Playing at Love." *Midwest Quarterly* 19 (1978): 313–29.

Brooke, Nicholas. *Shakespeare's Early Tragedies*. London: Methuen, 1968.

Bullough, Geoffrey. *Narrative and Dramatic Sources of Shakespeare*. London: Routledge & Kegan Paul, 1973.

Bush, Douglas. *English Literature in the Earlier Seventeenth Century*. Oxford: Clarendon, 1945.

Campbell, Lily. *Shakespeare's Tragic Heroes*. New York: Barnes & Noble, 1952.

Champion, Larry. *Shakespeare's Tragic Perspective*. Athens: University of Georgia Press, 1976.

Charlton, Henry B. *Shakespearean Tragedy*. Cambridge: Cambridge University Press, 1948.

Charney, Maurice. *Shakespeare's Roman Plays; The Function of Imagery in the Drama*. Cambridge: Harvard University Press, 1961.

Clemen, W. H. *The English Tragedy Before Shakespeare*. London: Methuen, 1961.

Colie, Rosalie. *Shakespeare's Living Art*. Princeton, N.J.: Princeton University Press, 1974.

Danby, John. "The Shakespearean Dialectic: An Aspect of *Antony and Cleopatra*." In *Poets on Fortune's Hill*. London: Faber & Faber, 1952.

Danson, Lawrence. *Tragic Alphabet*. New Haven: Yale University Press, 1974.

Eliot, T. S. *Elizabethan Essays*. London: Faber & Faber, 1953.

Ellis-Fermor, Una. *The Frontiers of Drama*. London: Methuen, 1948.

Evans, Bertrand. *Shakespeare's Tragic Practice*. Oxford: Clarendon, 1979.

Evans, Gareth L. *The Upstart Cow*. London: J. M. Dent, 1982.

Fiedler, Leslie A. *The Stranger in Shakespeare*. London: Croom Helm, 1972.

Goddard, Harold C. *The Meaning of Shakespeare*. Chicago: University of Chicago Press, 1951.

Harbage, Alfred, ed. *Shakespeare: The Tragedies*. Englewood Cliffs, N.J.: Prentice-Hall, 1964.

Harrison, George Bagshawe. *Shakespeare's Tragedies*. London: Routledge & Kegan Paul, 1951.

Holloway, John. *The Story of the Night*. London: Routledge & Kegan Paul, 1961.

Honigman, E. A. J. *Shakespeare: Seven Tragedies*. London: Macmillan, 1976.

Kernan, Alvin B., ed. *Modern Shakespearean Criticism*. New York: Harcourt, Brace & World, 1970.

Knight, George Wilson. *The Imperial Theme*. London: Methuen, 1951.

⸻. *The Wheel of Fire*. London: Methuen, 1949.

Knights, Lionel C. *Further Explorations*. London: Chatto & Windus, 1965.

Kott, Jan. *Shakespeare Our Contemporary*. London: Methuen, 1965.

Lawlor, John. *The Tragic Sense of Shakespeare*. New York: Harcourt Brace, 1960.

Leavis, F. R. "*Antony and Cleopatra* and *All for Love*." *Scrutiny* 5 (1936): 158–69.

MacCallum, M. W. *Shakespeare's Roman Plays and Their Background*. New York: Russell & Russell, 1967.

McElroy, Bernard. *Shakespeare's Mature Tragedies*. Princeton, N.J.: Princeton University Press, 1973.

Mason, Harold A. *Shakespeare's Tragedies of Love*. London: Chatto & Windus, 1970.

Muir, Kenneth. *Shakespeare the Professional and Related Studies*. Totowa, N.J.: Rowman & Littlefield, 1973.

Murry, John Middleton. *Shakespeare*. London: Jonathan Cape, 1936.

Nevo, Ruth. *Tragic Form in Shakespeare*. Princeton, N.J.: Princeton University Press, 1972.

Ridler, Anne, ed. *Shakespeare Criticism, 1935–1960*. Oxford: Oxford University Press, 1963.

Rosen, William. *Shakespeare and the Craft of Tragedy*. Cambridge: Harvard University Press, 1960.

Schanzer, Ernest. *The Problem Plays of Shakespeare*. New York: Schocken, 1963.

Schulman, Norma M. "A 'Motive for Metaphor': Shakespeare's *Antony and Cleopatra*." *Hebrew University Studies in Literature* 4 (1976): 154–74.

Shapiro, Michael. "Buying Her Greatness: Shakespeare's Use of Coterie Drama in *Antony and Cleopatra*." *The Modern Language Review* 77 (1982): 1–15.

Sisson, Charles J. *The Mythical Sorrows of Shakespeare*. Annual Shakespeare Lecture of the British Academy Lecture. London: H. Milford, 1932.

Snyder, Susan. *The Comic Matrix of Shakespeare's Tragedies.* Princeton, N.J.: Princeton University Press, 1979.

Spivack, Bernard. *Shakespeare and the Allegory of Evil.* New York: Columbia University Press, 1958.

Spurgeon, Caroline. *Shakespeare's Imagery.* Cambridge: Cambridge University Press, 1935.

Steiner, George. *The Death of Tragedy.* New York: A. Knopf, 1961.

Stoll, Elmer Edgar. *Art and Artifice in Shakespeare.* Cambridge: Cambridge University Press, 1933.

Traversi, Derek. *Shakespeare: The Roman Plays.* Stanford, Calif.: Stanford University Press, 1963.

Tucker, Kenneth. "Psychetypes and Shakespeare's *Antony and Cleopatra.*" *Journal of Evolutionary Psychology* 5 (1984): 176–81.

Vincent, Barbara C. "Shakespeare's *Antony and Cleopatra* and the Rise of Comedy." *English Literary Renaissance* 12, no. 1 (1982): 53–86.

Weis, René J. A. "*Antony and Cleopatra:* The Challenge of Fiction." *English* 32, no. 142 (1983): 1–14.

Whitaker, Virgil. *The Mirror up to Nature.* San Marino, Calif.: Huntington Library Publication, 1965.

Wilson, Harold S. *On the Design of Shakespearian Tragedy.* Toronto: University of Toronto Press, 1957.

Wolf, William D. " 'New Heaven, New Earth': The Escape from Brutality in *Antony and Cleopatra.*" *Shakespeare Quarterly* 33 (1982): 328–35.

Acknowledgments

"Infinite Variety: Uncertainty and Judgment in *Antony and Cleopatra*" by Janet Adelman from *The Common Liar: An Essay on* Antony and Cleopatra by Janet Adelman, © 1973 by Yale University. Reprinted by permission of Yale University Press.

" 'Nature's Piece 'Gainst Fancy': The Divided Catastrophe in *Antony and Cleopatra*" by Anne Barton from *An Inaugural Lecture* (to the Hildred Carlile Chair of English Literature in the University of London tenable at Bedford College, October, 1972) by Anne Barton, © 1973 by Anne Barton. Reprinted by permission.

"The Significance of Style" (originally entitled "*Antony and Cleopatra*: The Significance of Style") by Rosalie L. Colie from *Shakespeare's Living Art* by Rosalie L. Colie, © 1974 by Princeton University Press. Reprinted by permission of Princeton University Press.

"Mimesis and Modernity in *Antony and Cleopatra*" (originally entitled "Plays Within Plays: *Othello, King Lear, Antony and Cleopatra*") by Howard Felperin from *Shakespearean Representation: Mimesis and Modernity in Elizabethan Tragedy* by Howard Felperin, © 1977 by Princeton University Press. Reprinted by permission of Princeton University Press.

"Determined Things: The Case of *Antony and Cleopatra*" (originally entitled "Determined Things: The Case of the Caesars") by John Bayley from *Shakespeare and Tragedy* by John Bayley, © 1981 by John Bayley. Reprinted by permission of Routledge & Kegan Paul Ltd.

"Gender and Genre" (originally entitled "*Antony and Cleopatra*") by Linda Bamber from *Comic Women, Tragic Men: A Study of Gender and Genre in Shakespeare* by Linda Bamber, © 1982 by the Board of Trustees of the Leland Stanford Junior University. Reprinted by permission of the publishers, Stanford University Press.

"*Virtus* under Erasure" (originally entitled "*Antony and Cleopatra* [c. 1607]: *Virtus* under Erasure") by Jonathan Dollimore from *Radical Tragedy: Religion, Ideology and Power in the Drama of Shakespeare and his Contemporaries* by Jonathan Dollimore, © 1984 by Jonathan Dollimore. Reprinted by permission of the Harvester Press and the University of Chicago Press.

"Enter a Messenger" by Laura Quinney, © 1987 by Laura Quinney. Published for the first time in this volume. Printed by permission.

Index